THE BORDER

THE FUTURE OF POSTMODERNITY

THE BORDER

THE FUTURE OF POSTMODERNITY

Sergio Gómez Montero

SAN DIEGO STATE UNIVERSITY PRESS
Baja California Literature in Translation
San Diego, California
1994

The Border: The Future of Postmodernity by Sergio Gómez Montero is the third publication in San Diego State University Press's series "Baja California Literature in Translation." This book was supported by a generous grant from the Adams Humanities Fund administered through the San Diego State University Foundation, for which grateful acknowledgment is made.

FIRST EDITION

ISBN 1-879691-25-6

Translated from the Spanish by
Harry Polkinhorn, with the author

Cover image, "La Manina," by Carlos Coronado Ortega

Contents

Preface

Introduction, by Miguel Manríquez / 1

Animal Language and Human Language / 15

Language and the Border / 23

The Word and Reading-Writing on the Northern Border / 33

". . . What Is Language, Anyway?" / 43

National Symbols: Their Impact on the Border / 49

Chicanismo: Outline of a Theory / 69

Constructing Regional Cultures / 79

Folklore, Resistance, and the Border / 93

Cultural Politics in the Present: A Regional Focus / 105

Literature and History: Models to Provide / 121

An Unseizable Object: The Study of Literature / 127

The Literary Essay in the 29th State (Baja California) / 137

Literature and Regionalization in Sonora / 147

History and Regional Literature: An Endless Essay / 155

Border: Space, Time, and Postmodernity / 163

Acknowledgments: Some of these essays have been previously published. Grateful acknowledgment is made to:

"Language and the Border," *Tierra adentro,* 35/36 (July-December, 1983); ". . . What Is Language, Anyway?" *Ingenios para el estudio de la cultura,* Mexico City: UNAM, 1992, pp. 275-78; "*Chicanismo:* Outline of a Theory," *El oficio* (September, 1987), pp. 61-68; "*Constructing* Regional Cultures," *Cultura norte,* 9 (June-September, 1989); "Folklore, Resistance, and the Border, *La jornada semanal* (December 31, 1989); "Cultural Politics in the Present: A Regional Focus," *Esquina baja,* 13 (April-June, 1992); "Literature and History: Models to Provide," *Inventario,* 23 (October 13, 1991); "An Unseizable Object: The Study of Literature, *Contraseña,*(July 26, 1992); "The Literary Essay in the 29th State (Baja California)," *Inventario,* 3 (May 12, 1992); "An Endless Essay: History and Regional Literature;" "Border: Space, Time, and Postmodernity," *Sociedad y desierto,* Mexico City: UPN, 1992, pp. 91-102.

Preface

Searching for my reasons for bringing together the essays in this book, I have proposed to myself to write these lines not only about what is contained herein but also to offer some observations about what it means for me today to reflect upon and write about the Mexico-U.S. border. Thus, I would first like to point out that the writings gathered here are not all I have published on the subject. These essays, however, respond to a more precise logic: their intention is not to present a historical overview, whether or not incomplete, of what border literature and culture have recently been, but to place emphasis on the transitoriness and a sense of emergency in the current historical moment. Thus, what the border heralds today are "times of change," of which I speak about here. That is, a conjunction I consider strategic is identified, where continuity suffers substantial modifications and where the future, as it daily appears, can not be delineated with any certainty. Thus, the works assembled here are not chronologically ordered. Rather, their ordering responds to the "times of change."

Clearly, all borders are highly sensitive and fragile, as history confirms. But within this singularity one should separate out those moments of continuity from those of rupture. For me, the present is a time of rupture, perhaps within a context of continuity (this would have to be verified), which requires the elaboration of a hypothesis to understand what is happening.

It should be obvious that I do not intend to give an absolute response to this question. Rather, I am preoccupied, within a Foucauldian conception of social analysis, with establishing the particularity of the facts, their singularity, with the object of thus overcoming the domination that all processes of theoretical universalizing imply, which in principle evade reality and supposedly establish truths that are imposed through the perverse mechanisms of absolutism and dogmatism.

On the contrary, these essays lock onto concrete social realities and intend to evade transcendence and papal bulls. Neither are they the result of specific, determinate research, but rather are isolated sketches—although they are all the result of a profoundly dialectical conception of reality—of diverse themes whose common material of study is the culture and literature of the border between Mexico and the United States. These themes are intimately linked with each other and on joining them, I see them as seeking to penetrate into the inner meaning of the social life which is daily expressed in this geographic area. Their association, then, is not only of a casual nature, but one whose purpose it is to establish general principles that will permit us to accede—always through singularity and conjecture—to the emergent sense of reality of this area today.

Hence, the order of the presentation of the materials begins with language, because it is considered the base upon which reality is constructed, what could be called the code that permits us to travel free and unobserved through the region, beyond the grasp of the customhouse and migratory persecutions. The sequence continues with a focus on culture and personalities, in order thus to underscore the historicity of the reality of what is being referred to. The collection concludes with literature, in terms not of the past but of present immediacy with glimpses of the future.

More to the point—obsessed with Foucault—I think that an additional meaning of what I have brought together here has to do with the necessity of amplifying the frame of analysis of the social. I want to go beyond the purely economic, that is, the field of exploitation, in order more adequately to enter upon the still obscure and slippery terrain of domination and power, where territorial limits are erased, from the moment in which sovereignty and nationalism are established as values in and of themselves of the dominant hegemonies. In the same way these essays profile—through social analysis—what comprises subjection and how its mechanisms operate which emanate from contemporary technological development.

I would like to finish these comments by stressing the great debt I have to Harry Polkinhorn, Gabriel Trujillo Muñoz, Leobardo Saravia, Emily Hicks, Humberto Félix Berumen, Martha Sánchez

Soler, and Guillermo Gómez-Peña, among others, with whom through dialogue, fraternal discussion, friendship, and the interchange of experiences I have enriched my knowledge of the border between the U.S. and Mexico. Today this border is a routine obsession, in more than one sense my reason for being. I would especially like to mention my wife Norma, for the daily emotional support she always offers. My gratitude to all, and of course the deficiencies and possible errors in the material gathered here are mine alone.

Mexicali, Baja California
July, 1993

Introduction

Introducing a book makes possible reflections on a broad range of cultural phenomena: from those inscribed in stylistics and literary analysis to those that broach the search, through cultural activities, for the promotion of an author or institutional political legitimation. Another implication—less rational and closer to feeling—is that, in addition to whatever aesthetic consideration, the introduction should be a generous invitation to reading and reflection.

This also has another sense: to be confronted with the book brings with it the need for an assertive disposition, in other words, to approach the text with the desire to explore its claims, because the contrary irremediably fixes one's attention on the text's defects and absences. As a consequence, one is led to speak poorly of the author. (No doubt the ancient custom of inviting one's friends to write introductions stems from this.)

How do we avoid this ethical pitfall? How can we be faithful to friendship, to our readers, and to the search for knowledge without punishing ourselves? One of the most viable solutions is simply to postpone ideological battles with the author until tomorrow. The book in question then brings about an internal dialogue and—in the best of cases—an exchange of ideas with the author.

This ethical conflict resolved, I shall focus on the book's claims and, through the reflection they provoke, invite a reading and, to say it once and for all, to celebrate this new publication for the contributions it makes. To invite to reading, thus, is not to review the book's contents in any detail and, taking advantage of the text, to describe the greater part of its ideas through the insane custom of textual citations. This almost always causes potential readers to lose interest, conditioning their appreciation or at least prejudicing it towards the material in question. Rather, it has to do with offering an approach to possible readers, with learning new things through reflection on what these essays say. In the end, it deals with establishing a fruitful dialogue with the author. In the first instance, the works here published are the product of the intelligent practice of an office which has been matured by discipline and time until it has been converted into a way to perceive the world.

Once the meaning of these lines is established, we shall attend to those ideas which, in my judgment, cut diagonally through Sergio Gómez Montero's always sober and bold texts—in sum, to attend to what the texts say and don't say. The author's initial demarcation clearly identifies the parts which make up the whole: language, culture, and literature. In other words, he focuses the problem through three interrelated dimensions: discourse, a vision of the world, and literary practice as elements incorporated into the logic of power. Thus, Gómez Montero's methodological proposal is clear and precise: to establish general principles which—always through specificity and conjecture—permit us to arrive at the emergence of the present. Consequently, the contributions of the essays contained in this book initiate us into some of the author's thematic preoccupations.

i. Social Space and Symbol

Clearly, the first central theme which appears in this work is the border. If indeed border space is something more than a physical and three-dimensional entity, it is in the perception of this where the sensory and intellectual harnessing of the means becomes distinct and differentiated by the forms of apprehension of this space. That apprehension is presented here as a group of essays. For Gómez Montero subjects have images and schemes that are learned or indeed constructed, thereby establishing the subjective distances of time and space. In other words, physical perception is also mental, that is, symbolic perception, where subjects construct systems to manage the world through their experience. In other words, spatial categories represent a symbolic space which bears on regional culture.

The perception that this is auto-centric (the subject) or alo-centric (the object), in principle, implies the notion of a spatial form, the cognition of a space and time and an interiorizaton produced in the individual. The intellective seizing of geographic space is thus comprehension and knowledge. As a result, if intellectual reflection is also sensory grasping of the environment, then it is comprehension and knowledge.

In general, the author confirms the fact that we can think of the northern border as a geographic space in a period of redefinition in which all the elements of its structure are increasingly changing. To continue this tendency, it implies that processes of change in the ensemble of social life will be consolidated: from laws themselves to power relations with foreign nations and the rest of the country. This idea of change cuts diagonally through those analyses that focus on the border as a region debated as to its subjection to central power and its search for greater regional autonomy, or rather a conception of a border controlled by denationalized economic groups and another guided by authentic national democracies.[1]

In this sense, in Gómez Montero's texts the border region appears as a zone where the economic and political processes that sustain them generate culturally conflicting elements. Such effects are noticed on the international as well as the national plane in which the economic and political changes of position in the region are the most immediate effect. Growing industrialization of the border zones, the creation of *maquiladoras* as response to the low utilization of labor power in national industry, the United States' unilateral methods of controlling drug trafficking and migration, conflict in the use of international waters and political relations on the local level, population growth, and the consumption habits permeated by U.S. patterns, all configure the border as a social space in which significant cultural relations of dependence,[2] subordination, and inter-influence occur.

In this scenario of regional interaction, we find principally a process of assimilation in which there appear as fundamental determinants a contact with the economic flows of the southern United States, relative autonomy regarding national industry, and strong links regarding political sovereignty and sociocultural expressions of national identity. Such a model is producing an economic strategy based on the foreign market which implies a greater integration of the national economy and, of course, the border economy. The basic idea that permeates all the previous claims is that such considerations want to show the existing relations between those macroeconomic international phenomena and the internal economic, political, and social processes that modify the system of relations among the different cultural groups of society.

In this sense, a necessary condition for reflection on regional culture is to recognize that the social life of groups is determined by the production of material life, the organization of political life, and collective symbolic processes; all this is given shape through nationalism, cultural heterogeneity, and the structures of cultural domination. Regional culture contains characteristic determining elements such as the processes of cultural penetration based on technology, industrialization, local and national power groups, language and its aesthetic realizations, ways of life and consumption habits, growing urbanization, and phenomena related to identity-formation.

Another of the prisms through which reflection is sustained is the centrality of language in culture. The theme of language is a fundamental part of Gómez Montero's project. His conception of language comprises the potential of discovering its expressive riches, its symbolic plane, and how it facilitates communication. Thus, Gómez Montero reminds us also that language is an aesthetic construct, that is, literature. The natural consequence, then, is that for the reflection of culture, language and literature are simultaneously nodal points and instruments of analysis.

Seen in this way, literature is an ensemble of relations among distinct ideas about the world. In this sense, the author maintains that literary practice not only establishes some relations, but it discovers others and forms structures to transmit to us ideas about life. In this tenor, literature, as much a system of ideas, is sustained precisely in a linking of connections of meaning as well as formally in a language that serves, finally, to express and know the world configured by customs, behavior, valorizations, and symbols, that is, the elementally human.

For this semiotic process to occur (or at least so assumes the author), a communicative act occurs—or at least an intention—which inexorably leads us to think about interlocution, that is, culture as dialogical relation. Therefore, in this perspective an aesthetic fact is an entirety of relations of meaning that has, among its multiple determinants, the following relations: a) the linguistic norm/literary form; b) perception of the world/internalization of the artist; and c) aesthetic structure/symbolic meaning. Such relations necessarily lead to a binomial: perception of the world/structure of meaning. Better put, if language establishes relations of meaning, then literature has a multiplier effect on meanings in a given space and time.

Nevertheless, such bold claims lack the other ingredient already mentioned: dialogical relation. If we begin with the consideration that literature is a *form of knowledge* with different but complementary methods to those of science and philosophy, then we have to accept that, as a form of knowledge, literature has four fundamental relations: logical, historical, epistemological, and dialogical. For reasons of space and disciplinary perversion, I will only take up the last. The dialogical relation refers to logos as Reason and as word. On the one hand, logos as word refers to the existence of the possible interlocutor; on the other hand, it implies a form of articulation of knowledge, that is, word and symbol.

In this sense, for Gómez Montero logos (in its Platonic acceptation) implies communicative interaction and, at the same time, significative content, that is, expressivity ("all that *signify* expresses, all that *express* signifies"): the intellection of a signified as precondition of the communication of a symbol. Formulated expressly: regional literatures as symbolic forms, intersubjective relation. Here we see the author's pertinent proposals: he calls for the creation of workshops for the spread of language and artistic creation, research into reading-writing on the border, the educational process related to language, all seen as factors for recognizing identity-formation.

The author refers to the fact that historicity in the literary writer is a trans-subjective process that acts as historical situational conditioner of a vision of the world. In other words, historicity in literature grows precisely from interlocution and the commitment to elaborate mental structures congruent with the world experienced by social subjects: border residents and Chicano culture.

ii. Knowledge and Power

Gómez Montero brings up another fundamental question that, in my judgment, is found implicit in his texts. For the analysis of research in the field of culture one must begin with the idea that in this activity are found different mediations which determine as much the theoretical plane as conditions of production of same. This section is made up of three dimensions that turn out to be central for initiating discussion.

The first relation refers to the socioeconomic conditions that influence the disciplinary configuration of the study of culture. A second moment is that which bears on the plane of the relations between culture and the Mexican State, that is, between knowledge and power. The third relation, more concrete and immediate, is that which broaches the internal dynamic of the cultural phenomenon as object of study.

Among the multiplicity of mediations in the production of knowledge are to be found those inscribed in the principle processes characterizing contemporary societies. Given this consideration, we establish a first dimension of analysis: socioeconomic conditions. In whichever discipline, it is already a commonplace to refer to the 1980s as characterized by the *new world order* generated through two simultaneous processes of still inconclusive change: the restructuring of the capitalist system on the world level as a form of reorganizing the already extensive recession initiated at the end of the 1970s; and the reincorporation into the logic of capital of those societies organized through *real socialism* and the consequent collapse of their governments and economies.

In this sense, it seems ingenuous not to accept that these changes have significantly impacted the distinct intellectual fields in their entirety and theories of culture in specific. The effects in the disciplines are of diverse order: from those that seek to rediscover their rationale in the remote past to those that declare the exhaustion of Marxist ideas ascribing them to the neoliberal model;[3] not to forget, of course, the discussion centered on the end of modernity and the arrival of postmodernity.

This deals not only with the growing globalization of economies but also with ways of life, symbolic referents, and knowledge. We refer to changes in ethical, aesthetic, and identity-oriented values generated through the transformation of material conditions of existence. This process brings an effect in the forms of hierarchization and priorities within knowledge in general and within research into cultural phenomena in particular.

To reflect on the aspects mentioned above implies the recurrence of concrete referents of national reality. In other words, reflection begins with the fact that faced with the current scenario of the Free Trade Agreement, we are in a situation of interculturality which implies the recognition not only of the differences between cultures but also of unequal forms of appropriation of the cultural elements on the part of groups in three different countries.

Seen in this way, the cultural question refers to the analysis of inter-determinations among the relations of power existing in the State, economic processes, social and political life, configuration of ideologies, and the symbolic specter generated in such a dynamic. Therefore, these dimensions determine the conformation of identities as far as expression of order and the meaning of a Nation. The question of culture appears, then, as a field which also presupposes projects on the infrastructural level regarding the so-called culture industry. Given the peculiarities of the national culture industry and the predictable intensification of contacts with North American culture—

whose expressions, while increasingly fragmented by the characteristics of its population, are paradoxically unified by values of consumption, efficiency, competence, technification, and obsolescence—we are presented with a profile in which the dominant trait is the lack of regional politics for culture, creating a disadvantageous context for confronting the differences of these cultural models.

To put it bluntly: *the processes of globalization of ideas, symbols, values, and knowledge produced by advanced societies determine the development of the themes of research and the different forms of interpretation of the world of life.*

A second dimension of analysis to which Gómez Montero leads us for reflection on culture refers to the relation between culture and the State, that is, between knowledge and power. In this order of ideas, the contemporary State is also borne up through culture, in order to exercise its functions through strategies of cultural promotion linked to the administration of public resources, the necessities of social control, and the legitimating of policies that seek to guarantee social stability. Thus, we encounter in Gómez Montero a permanent preoccupation with the cultural politics of the State as characterized by the centralism of decisions, the ambiguity of state interventions, selectivity towards cultural groups, inequality in the distribution of resources, and the bureaucratic control of official actions.

Theorization of the origin and nature of the State has, of course, different levels of explanation, different points of view, and distinct appreciations that seek to project the dynamic of power. Nevertheless, in Gómez Montero's view, the State and its exercise of power regarding culture are understood differently. A multidimensional conception of the State is offered by means of which an ensemble of structural relations is presented which cannot be reduced to only apparatuses and institutions, or to ideological amalgamations, or simply to political practices.

In the case of our country, it is a fact that the State has been transformed. By different circumstances that there is no point in summarizing here, the author claims that the State is very different from the foundational State that emerged from the armed conflict of 1910, whose distinct traits have been gradually transformed by the crisis of the 1980s, international imperatives, and new relations of power. These essential characteristics—we all recognize them—are presidentialism, the existence of a State party, a degraded nationalist ideology, alliances, and increasingly pointless social policies.

The new Mexican State—complex and contradictory by nature—is a prism whose fundamental dimensions are the processes of economic integration, the emergence of new corporate bodies, the reform of the State, ambiguous and relative modernization, and a sanitized and selective democracy with its forms of political control, authoritarianism as governmental modality, exclusionary arrangements, and the permanent politics of consummated facts.

In this order of ideas, "complexity and differentiation that Mexican society achieved in this decade [the 1980s] indicate that the principal vectors of the country come from the direction of society. Faced with this situation, the Mexican State confronts one of its principal challenges: to leave behind its corporate and authoritarian profile in order to respond to new social demands and economic necessities, that is, to be able to govern a pluralistic society"[4] in which cultural heterogeneity is one of its most distinctive traits.

In the case of Mexico, the relation between State and culture has passed through distinct phases in the period 1910 to 1990 which comprise relations of subordination, amplification, and/or reduction of the margins of participation, the adjustments of the programs of official culture to national development, and the impulse of the politics of coordination and rationalization that strengthen the bases for a greater political control of the responsible apparatuses of culture promoted by the State. These characteristics frame the State-culture relation where organizational aspects stand out from the cultural institutions, cultural politics, the norms that rule such relations and the state actions over culture as far as these form part of a process of political and social advantage.

These mediations displace the focal points of analysis of research on culture. If earlier in the research the point of reference is a State reduced only to apparatuses and institutions, or to ideological amalgamations and practical politics inscribed in macro-phenomena, today one conceives of this State as an ensemble of structural relations, that is, the modern State as a multidimensional unity. It brings as an effect the privileging of that investigation with a micro-dynamic vision of political society where the cultural question is intersected by the essential dynamics of civil society.

In other words, *research on culture should proceed to the analysis of local spheres, ways of life, consumption habits, symbols and values, social movements, self-creating experiences, and the ensemble of those daily mechanisms of social reproduction in which subjects are producers of cultural practices and experiences.* In such a sense, Gómez Montero's works lead to the necessity of revising fundamental theoretical suppositions, to broach critically the conception itself of culture and, as a consequence, to establish the possible and immediate character and orientation of this reflection on regional culture centered on the qualitative dimensions of society.

One of the loose ends that the author leaves—perhaps, one hopes, for later books—is the third level of analysis. It is that which refers to the internal dynamic of research on culture, that is, the ensemble of mediations which determine the theoretical-methodological planes, as well as the central ideas that animate these disciplinary fields. Gómez Montero is clearly occupied with a series of mediations such as the political situation, economic interests, ideological debates, as well as the priorities established as a function of the necessities of social development in the region as well as of the life of cultural research itself. This preoccupation leads to the proposition of emphasizing the existence of different factors of national and international character that determine some objects and objectives of research to the detriment of others.

In this order of ideas, the methodological discussion is left hanging in the sense that, beyond the thematic hierarchizations, it is important to show that culture, as activity of investigation, shares problems with social research in its entirety. Culture is not an analytical object that possesses a defined theoretical and conceptual body given its disciplinary genealogy. As a consequence, one of the possible escape routes, in my judgment, is trans-disciplinarity as an essential condition for the deepening of knowledge in research on culture.

In this view, we run across theoretical-methodological questions of the first order which constitute, perhaps, the central point for discussion with the author of this book.[5] The first consideration refers to the disciplinary boundaries of culture; if indeed these boundaries are determined and adapted to political, social, and economic structures in process of change, then cultural research in the future should be to broach from macro-analysis the social and cultural transformations through regional contexts.

In other words, we find that the study of cultural phenomena has been basically oriented on the analysis of these in stable societies that currently are found in processes of transition. This implies a revision of the theoretical-methodological schemes of cultural research with the proposition of generating pertinent, timely, creative, and above all appropriate research to give answers to the phenomena of societies with an accelerated transition in their institutions, value systems, cultural relations, and identity-formation changes. A third moment of this question is that the existence of new phenomena in processes of transition as well as the development of recent models for the study of nonlinear phenomena—irreversibly stemming from the hard sciences—give to cultural research the opportunity to explore interdisciplinarity and transdisciplinarity.

In this view, culture is seen as an intellectual activity that generates the production of new knowledge transcending its own thematic boundaries. Within these boundaries are found processes such as globalization and the changes it works in political, social, and cultural maps; relations between demographic phenomena with economic and social components faced with ethnic, urban, and industrial processes associated with cultural movements; culture and its relations with aesthetic and linguistic aspects, but also identity, consumption, sovereignty, politics, and social ethics.

iii. Colophon

Gómez Montero reflects on distinct themes related among themselves. These have the admirable quality of broaching fundamental questions for cultural life in regional space. This book bears on the multiple artistic and cultural expressions that occur in the periphery of a centralized State and its exercise of power. The texts in their entirety are the committed search to interrelate feelings and ideas, sensibilities and perceptions that the border dweller has constructed, always in a process of definition and change. Although he recognizes the existence of micro-regions, the author does not scorn the real integration and participation of these in the national project.

If indeed the concepts that appear in the texts are not finished and call for further elaboration, it is clear that the author departs from theories that question passivity and statism of these theoretical proposals on culture which do not consider the evolution and development of ideas on the plane of history. In any case, the richness of this work stems from the fact that it permits us to rethink and, in the best of cases, to criticize those cultural conceptions based on or sustained by innocuous, feeble, and at the same time questionable conceptions that only pretend to cut from the same cloth the diversity of artistic and cultural expressions of the different regions.

Finally, Gómez Montero's book demonstrates, once again, that from academic activity is produced knowledge and, at the same time, critical debates are offered that are found implicated in the political order and the permanent search of democratic life so feared by some. To say it once and for all: the vision that Gómez Montero brings us is sustained by the unavoidable and everyday vital necessity to construct the art of *making the desirable possible*.

Miguel Manríquez D.
Hermosillo, Sonora

Notes

[1]Cf. Bernardo Gonzalez-Arechiga and José Carlos Ramirez, "Definición y perspectivas de la región fronteriza, in *Estudios sociológicos,* No. 23 (May-August, 1990). In this article, the authors construct seven "base interpretations" in which there appear as factors of change: a) the rules of regional games; b) the commercial opening of the country and macro-economic policies; c) the evolution of the world market; d) regional legislation and binational agreements that affect the border; e) the conditions of accumulation of capital; f) the endogenous processes of the region that bear on the capacity to negotiate (manage); and g) the growing competition of the border with other regions of the country for the advantages of the process of economic opening.

[2]Mario Ojeda in his book *Alcances y límites de la política exterior de México* (Mexico City: Colmex, 1976) characterizes the relations of dependence as "a series of links of the political and economic type that are formal and extra-formal, which constitute direct and indirect conduct so that hegemonic potency can put pressure with better effect and above all with discretion, limiting the freedom of action of the governments involved." p. 9.

[3]If indeed the term *neoliberal* is already a universally accepted convention, we believe, following Pradilla Cobos, that it has rather to do with a *neoconservative* tendency now that this ideology, sustained formally by liberalism, does not contain its democratic, nationalist, and anti-imperialist values. The concrete sources must be located in economic and political thought of the period of consolidation of monopoly capitalism of the end of the 19th century and beginnings of the 20th.

[4]Jorge Alonso, Alberto Aziz, et al., *El nuevo estado mexicano,* Mexico City: Nueva Imagen, 1992, pp. 9, T. iv.

[5]Lourdes Arizpe's article "Los desafíos intelectuales en las ciencias sociales," (bulletin of the Mexican Council of Social Sciences, Number 6 [Mexico City, 1993]) is amply illustrative. This material

has guided my reflections on research in culture given the amplitude and depth with which the problematics of the social sciences are established and which are applied to culture.

Animal Language and Human Language

For a long time—at least since Darwin—doubts over the genetic linkages that exist among human language and animal language have been kept out of the discussion. Today, movies like *Gorillas in the Mist* clearly illustrate the existence and meaning of these linkages.

Moreover, how we understand language, above all its differentiating function, calls for serious reflection. In a strict sense, language can be called an "instrument of communication," indistinctly utilized, although not equally so, by people and animals. Really, then, when one wants to deal more with this theme today than to speak of redundancies, one must look into new areas. If they are very difficult to capture, they help considerably to enrich the study of the material. This brief work broaches several essential points in this regard. At the end a short bibliography is given which was the foundation for the elaboration of the material.

1

I begin by considering language—that of humans and of animals—as an autonomous but not isolated entity. Hence, I want to speak of it as an "instrument of communication," to be able to locate it in a broader referential context which permits removing it from the purely linguistic sphere in order to insert it into another field close to linguistics but not confused with it. I refer here to communication, understood moreover as a process of energy necessary to matter to reproduce itself. In fact, communication in this sense is energy, and in another sense all processes of communication in turn require language as a basic instrument of concretion, as part of their chain or the circuit through which they express themselves. Here I cite Bühler: "Language is related to instruments; it also belongs among the utensils of life, is an *organon* like a real utensil, an intermedial material thing foreign to the body; as instrument, language is a *shaped intermediary*" (1985: 12) (my emphasis).

In such a brief discussion, I cannot speak here about how communication as energy is expressed in the inorganic or in less complex living organisms than we. Contemporary physics and botany have much to say on this score. Systems theory applied to these fields has contributed essential facts. And it is precisely in good measure systems theory which has helped us more rigorously to understand that which could be called the necessity of communication as a basis for the development of animals and human beings.

The problem, thus, is in explaining what is understood by communication. Generic communication, without adjectives. In this way, I want to begin with movement—the dialectic—as one of the blind spots of the concretion of matter, always remembering that matter and movement are both fundamentally energy. As energy is neither creation nor destruction, the metaphor that allows us to approximate its definition more closely is that of the sphere or circle (a reading of Parmenides helps considerably to enter upon the theme of the finite/infinite), but not in the way that repetition continues from the point that is reproduced in order to return to find how it was in the beginning; but as the point which is to cease to be, that is, which moves in order to change. There the existence of the other ineluctably gives concretion to the circuit. The link between the one and the other is language continually codified and decodified, insofar as the circle is the circuit of communication. In fact, then, the existence of the one and the other always of necessity generates the existence of communication and finally of language.

As an instrument of communication, language is concrete and is codified. That is, using Aristotelian jargon, language has essence, and its form always responds to a code (rules of decoding). Once decodified, language becomes information. What the circuit of communication produces is information, concretized in a language (ceaselessly codified and decodified).

Both as energy, dialectics and matter—from the simplest to the most complex—generate circuits of communication perfectly delimited and of an almost infinite variety. In this variety are inscribed both human and animal languages.

2

The necessities of reproduction of matter in fact are those that fix the parameters within which language is generated. In some such sense the differences among languages are given by the different ways that matter takes to reproduce itself. Hence, simply referring to the animal, we can observe marked differences between the language which birds use and that used by ants; and even among birds there are differences, because the conditions of reproduction of a pigeon are different from those of a duck, so that their needs of communication and elaboration of languages are also different.

And following the Darwinian scheme, we note that among the animals the primates are closest to the human species in terms of development. It is not by chance that there are similarities—some very close indeed—between the primates' circuits of communication and those of humans, and finally, clearly, of their "languages" at the level of gesture and sound. Why? Basically because some of the processes of reproduction of their species are superficially similar; that is, both groups fundamentally respond to common motives that thus generate similar informational charges.

On the one hand, the motivations life/death, love/hate, gregarious instinct, play, feeding, and, on the other hand, superficially similar physical structures necessarily give rise to similar circuits of communication and to languages that in good measure are identified, but are differentiated in particular, because the primate does not abstract. Its thought is very rudimentary as it has not yet been able to distance itself from the senses, which continue being the basis of its reproduction.

Here it is necessary to forget anthropomorphism as a referential point of language, in order to understand that the above-mentioned instrument is generic to different species (in fact, to all species) and that, therefore, the problem of its study is not found in the fact of comparing language X with human language, but in defining circuits of communication to identify language in them in order then to define which are the principal characteristics of this language, at the time that the subject possessing language is defined and the circuit of communication in which subject and language are operating. There is not much point, then, in a Darwinian conception of how human language and animal language are linked. What is important is to establish the presence of both and the central characteristics of their nature and functions.

The border—that point where there is contact but also where difference is perceived—between animal language (particularly that of primates) and human language establishes, as Bühler says, that no common animal life exists without means of directing the collective conduct of the community; there is no community without *interchange of signs,* which in the kingdom of living animal beings is as ancient as the *interchange of materials,* and this means of direction, which we can exactly observe, is the prehuman analog of language. Later, Bühler says an interchange of very organized materials among members of a living animal community would be absolutely impossible without an exchange of signs. In this regard, says the German critic, it is necessary to erect a biologically well founded theory of language and then to realize yet one more amplification of its horizon.

3

How to amplify the horizon? Bühler never says, and as I said at the beginning of this discussion, one of the polemical points of the study of language today, if in fact no one denies the existence of a common trunk—materiality and sign, which Bühler called *semantology* or the general theory of the sign—it is evident that from this precarious base the study of human language has taken off in different directions. These have as much to do with the four governing theses of the oft-cited Bühler as with Saussure's positivism of dualities and oppositions, with Martinet's double articulation, with Gorski's prerequisites—physical, biological, and psychological—with Piaget's psychogenetic maturing by stages, or finally with Chomsky's generative grammar (and I skip over names and theories such as Vygotski, Bruner, the Prague School, etc.).

In essence, the contemporary study of human language is a continually expanding field that would seem never to be closed. It repeatedly returns to its common roots as a way of protecting itself each time it would seem to be leaving its sources, whether to link itself unnecessarily with history, physics (Lenneberg 1981), psychology, or with the field that comprises semiology, semantics, and the philosophy of language. All these are disciplines that have as their matter the study of language, or at least they utilize language as a point of reference, without until now a response having been universalized about what human language is.

Any definition with which one wants to work is insufficient to establish with clarity and relevance what is understood as language, or what *should* be understood by it. But, in fact, if no definition escapes materiality and signification, all enter into conflict through it from the moment in which it becomes impossible to establish with enough certainty the functions and implications of human language. And conflicts occur, for example, from that moment in which language takes on weight in the interior of almost all theories, whether oral language and to a lesser degree writing, thereby noticeably reducing the communicative potentiality of human beings. Hence, the study of language should depart from this potentiality; it is here that the oral occupies a place of significance. In this way, when we speak of human language normally reference is made to the oral expression of signs, and connotes, therefore, one of the multiple circuits through which people are able to communicate. Thus, when studying oral language we must first delimit what it is and where it is located with regard to communication.

In such a fashion, perhaps Merani is right (following Gorski and Tavants) when on speaking of human language he establishes its tightly interrelated fields of study: people's phonic capacity to produce sounds; the psychological correlation that occurs between language and thought; the significant essence of language in itself; and the historical character of language. If Merani does not mention these as limits to the oral, we in fact *are* proposing this as our initial basis of reflection and analysis. In this way, a complete, broad series of subfields would be opened up inside each one of these four fields, facilitating the study of oral language among people.

References

Benjamin, Walter. *Sobre el programa de la filosofía futura y otros ensayos*. Caracas,Venezuela: Monte Avila, 1970.

Bühler, Karl. *Teoría del lenguaje*. Madrid, Spain: Alianza Universidad, 1985.

Gorski, D. P. *Historia de la escritura*. Mexico City: Grijalbo, 1962.

Lenneberg, Eric H. *Fundamentos biológicos del lenguaje*. Madrid, Spain: Alianza Universidad, 1981.

Merani, Alberto L. *El lenguaje*. Mexico City: Grijalbo, 1979.

Rousseau, Jean Jacques. *Ensayo sobre el origen de las lenguas*. Mexico City: Fondo de Cultura Económica, 1984.

Salado Aquino, José Manuel, ed. *El lenguaje en la novela*. Mexico City: UPN, 1987.

Schaff, Adam. *Lenguaje y acción humana.* Madrid, Spain: A. Redondo, 1969.

Language and the Border

> Cooley had a beautiful voice when he spoke with passion.
>
> —D. H. Lawrence, *Kangaroo*

Introduction

Usually in those countries like ours where the mixing of races has not been able to erase either the surviving ethnic manifestations of colonialism, or has imposed common patterns upon the nation as a whole, there is also found the uneasiness that comes of erasing the cultural differences that have endured. In the case of the ethnic, there are appeals to modernity (imposing civilization on barbarism, it is argued). In the case of the regional, we see attempts to reduce the differences that geography and society (or deeper cultural roots) have brought about to one model called national culture. This "culture," they claim, is able to unify the above-mentioned differences (or at least this is how it is conceived), in order thus chauvinistically to confront the "foreigner."

In the face of this tendency, there exists another (as happens in the case of contemporary Mexico), which admits the existence of different cultures and argues in favor of their enduring. More than anything else, pluriculturalism today is a dissatisfaction that has not been able to define its theoretical premises. On the one hand, it is still a subordinate tendency in the interior of the dominant ideology, and, on the other hand, it is an emerging cultural politics whose objective is to support the recycling of the ruling economic model in its ambition to overcome the centralism that today caps and limits it. Ideologically, pluriculturalism would correspond to the decentralization that is being urgently promoted these days. Seen more as emerging politics, which occurs moreover within a situation of acute social crisis, pluriculturalism is an open option, in whose process of definition there can also intervene the emerging social classes or those marginalized by society (the working class, the national and social minorities).

In such a context, lacking an express politics of language, the State in Mexico has tended more toward the first variable mentioned here ("national culture") than toward the second, which would consider a priority more the preservation of languages than their unification. By preserving languages we understand the analysis of the circuits of communication sustained in language (in both its synchronic and diachronic aspects), not through a process of confrontation with an ideal, nonexistent, national tongue, but giving these languages the ability to survive to the degree that the reality which brings them about itself survives.

The Northern Border

A special region of the country (one need only review history to have a closer idea of this specialness), the northern border of Mexico today, it can once again be said, is one of the strategic regions of the nation. Without denying the characteristics that are proper to each zone of the border (zones that tentatively can be delimited in terms of state territories), one can claim that the entire northern border region of Mexico presents a group of common characteristics, among which the following stand out:

> the lack of horizontal communication: a border dweller from one state is unknown to the border dweller of the neighboring state;
>
> the demographic formation of the cities is the result, primarily, of massive processes of migration, an overwhelming phenomenon in the population sphere but which has not been able to erase the specialness proper to the original inhabitants of the region;
>
> the tight economic interdependence which occurs between the two sides of the border and which today in particular is generating phenomena of increasing complexity (the interdependence is asymmetrical, which means that the economic, political, and ideological activities on the Mexican side are subordinate to those in the neighboring country);
>
> the alienating impact caused by the mass media of communication on both sides of the border;
>
> the resistance which the Mexican and Mexican-origin youth in particular show (those who belong to the lower and lower-middle classes of the population) toward the hegemony of the capitalist consumer culture, which has lead them to vindicate apparently obsolete and marginal forms of life and to create specific codes of communication; and
>
> a profound interrelation among the customs and modes of life of a Mexican border people and that of people of Mexican origin who originated in the border states of the U.S.A.

Culture and Language

Language is one of the basic factors of the identity of a people. The others are territory, customs and beliefs, and social organization. That is, language is one of the elements that overcomes differences, making possible a blending, something that gives unity and reason for being.

All language influences thought, and correlatively thought exercises its influence on language. In this way, a tight, indissoluble connection is established between both entities. In a certain sense, the development of language should be conceived as a function of the degree of development achieved by thought. More as a humanizing factor, language is developed and conditioned by the predominant social structures in a determinate historical stage. Thus it acquires ideological characteristics that lead it to fulfill functions that overdetermine its strictly semiotic task. In other words, language serves as an instrument of domination in the context of class struggle. Also within such a context, however, it can serve as an instrument of liberation.

In this way, all processes that look to preserve language should take into consideration at least three factors:

culture, and the role language plays in it;

the relation between thought and language, understood as the field in which language undergoes different changes; and

the historical context, understood as expression of social forces which on initiating language transform it.

Language and the Border

In the case of border dwellers, educational factors indicate that the demand for basic education is being satisfactorily met, and at the higher levels it is very comparable to the national mean. We should point out, however, that these indicators do not capture relevant aspects with regard to what is referred to as the use and manipulation of language (these aspects are of course not the property of the border but here they attain particular relevance). Among these aspects I note the following:

> Deficiencies exist in the teaching of materials linked to the teaching of language and literature, and libraries and bookstores in the region are scarce. Thus, reading, as an exercise practiced by the masses, focuses primarily on "cheap" literature: anecdotes, comics, sports pages.
>
> On the northern border different national "dialects" coexist, thereby making possible the existence of a linguistic "market" of significant richness.
>
> As part of the self-generated processes of defense of cultural identity, there are a series of goals and paralanguages (labeling Chicano language as "*chola*"), which correspond to cultural minorities, whose impact is growing on everyday speech.
>
> Border life generates a constant linguistic interchange, which indiscriminately introduces neologisms and anglicisms into everyday speech. This results from the economic relations of interdependence and the impact of the mass media of communication (in large part of North American origin).
>
> For youth, and in general for those who are fascinated with writing, there are few possibilities for satisfying this hunger, for setting it in motion and finding means with the goal of expression.

> All the above contribute gradually to a condition in which certain values of national society itself and of regional culture suffer deterioration and decay.

Language and Economy

Decontextualized, language would be an inert body (a tongue that tends towards death) whose social function would be null. Conceived more than anything as an instrument of communication, language must be understood through knowing the factors that dynamize it, that is, in which context it acquires validity and which elements make up this context.

Thus, if one cannot deny that an important part of its vitality is found by language in itself, the truth is that this is not the basic cause that preserves and maintains it. Thus, it is not its function as code that grants permanence and validity to language. It is, rather, the relation established between language, in its acceptation as process of communication, and the social sphere. This standard grants validity and permanence: when a language stops being socially useful it changes into a dead language.

Now then, the substantial weight of social processes falls back on the economic. From there, then, all language, whether natural or specialized, can be spoken of in more than one sense under the rubric of economy as a determining factor of linguistic dynamics. Valid language is therefore that which best expresses the interests proper to the dominant economic facts. In the case of the border, the above is the premise that explains the existence, for example, of a marked syncretism between Spanish and English (here the above-mentioned principle of asymmetry also operates). By contrast, the existence of certain metalanguages, or ciphered languages, corresponds to sectors of the population (*cholos*) which resist incorporation into the dominant social order.

It would simplify things, of course, to reduce the emphasis of the problematic of language on the border to a registration of the number of anglicisms used in daily life. The problem, however, is much more complex and should be analyzed through looking at the development that languages have had in a region where the economy has produced the manifestation of at least the following three linguistic phenomena of singular importance:

> the existence of a broad market of dialects generated by migratory processes;
>
> the syncretism that operates, asymmetrically, at the level of language, between neighboring regions; and
>
> the existence of parallel dialects, codified in a singular manner that resist and oppose the dominant linguistic model.

Workshops, Language, and Literature

The formal manifestations of language are presented in three great fields: the scientific, literary, and colloquial. In the first case, the specificity of the semiotic system is sustained in the rigidity of the relations that are established among their components (transmitter, receiver, and code), by virtue of the fact that these components should correspond in a strict way to the function that it is up to them to discharge. The teaching of this kind of language requires specific and methodical modes of instruction.

Literary language searches in its different manifestations for the transformation of immediate reality, with the object of imparting a particular vision of events in order to present to these last removed from its original categories. This creative act leads to and experiments in and with the informational system, submitting it to the designs of the subject who acts on it. In this case, language always responds to the development achieved by the individual who utilizes it and therefore is conditioned, first, by the social and ideological position of the subject, and, second, by the fluctuations that economic and political conditions impose on it as realized in the linguistic act.

Colloquial language, vast and complex in itself, should be conceived in the apparently narrow frame of the role that it plays in originating linguistic diffusion. The more immediate store of what is disposed over in colloquial language is found to exercise daily communication. Likewise, given the recent "discovery" of its value as such, colloquial language is the first to resent influences which originate, for example, whether captured first in the impact that the mass media of communication have on the most diverse sectors of the population. This impact modifies not only language but also the conduct of the members of these sectors, trying to sensitize their conduct so that it adopts as its own fictitious necessities and forms of being and of acting that injure human nature.

Under these assumptions, the literature workshop is one valid option so that, in certain young people, a kind of dissatisfaction can be channeled through writing, consolidating and reaffirming their cultural identity, redeeming singular aspects of this culture (a culture that rejects and confronts the dominant capitalist culture). More than anything, a literature workshop simultaneously projects the dissatisfaction of some youth through the medium of literature and is a center of artesanal work in different senses. First, the workshop is a place where the office of writing is learned collectively (at the level of literary and colloquial language). This office of writing is conceived as the knowledge of language understood in its function as communicational instrument. The workshop participant, on familiarizing himself to the greatest possible degree with this instrument, should construct with it different products (language is thus transformed from an object into a product). Second, the experience of writing permits the user of the workshop to open himself up to an option of a different kind of knowledge of reality. And third, in this way the personal development of the human being is consolidated.

We speak here of a teaching of language (of human language and how it emerges in an immediate way from the social environment) and of literature that puts people in relation with their daily reality, that is, a teaching that humanizes, granting the capacity to the human being to perfect the mechanisms by means of which one communicates with others, with oneself, and with the "other" in general. This teaching in a basic way finds in written language its favorite vehicle of expression. Supported by reading, this kind of teaching also facilitates oral communication. Finally, it contributes to epistemological processes, seeking to give people a critical and self-critical sense.

The Workshop: An Option

To escape the dynamic of the economy, language, just like other cultural manifestations, cannot hope that the economy in its totality will change (that is, that the social system will change). More than that, if, as happens on the border, the preoccupation with improving the quality of language understood as a circuit of communication is scarce or null, then neither the transmitter, the code, nor the receiver will motivate a better discharging of language's social function

The proposal that is made here to attempt this improvement implies a work that basically culminates in the creation of one or various centers of linguistic and literary specialization (centers of the academic study of language and literature).

Thus, at the base of the pyramid would be situated those that are here called "workshops for the diffusion of language," whose specific function would be centered on the best use and manipulation of colloquial language. The person attending the sessions of these workshops would try to familiarize himself with writing and literature, strengthen his cultural awareness to outfit him for the use of language as an instrument of communication. Eventually, he would be able to build an interest in perfecting himself in the use and manipulation of language. These workshops would operate in those centers where the handling of oral and written language is expedited (where literacy is common) and where, therefore, the fashioning of certain sophisticated products (a bulletin, a newspaper wall, a speech, a flier) would be possible. Such workshops, therefore, would be located in centers of community development and schools of the middle and upper levels.

On the second level of the pyramid would be the "workshops of literary creation," where, preferably, literary language would be the focus (its use, its handling, its creative dynamics). Moreover, these workshops would be based on an outline of literary readings ruled by a plan with the object that thus reading would feed back into writing in such a way that the characteristic office of literary writing would be furthered. We depart here from the assumption that literary writing is practiced spontaneously in whatever type of society (in whatever sector of it), moreover, that it is one of its daily practices.

The activities of the two workshops mentioned are conceived as a group of communicating vases. From the workshop of the spread of language members emerge for the workshop of literary creation, whose members, in turn, return to the other workshop but now as leaders of it. Finally, linguistic and literary activities thus impelled, these workshops would form the basis to permit a better specialization of reading and of writing, in terms that technical, specialized studies of language and literature can be realized in Baja California, at least for the near future.

Workshop activities are only one such process required to impel the regional development of language and literature. This job should see itself supported, in its basics, by plans that promote the creation of libraries, publications, bookstores, and interchanges of a cultural character. A society that is capable of reading and writing is a society that is known, that knows its defects, its limitations, and its potentialities. When a society cannot know (cannot read or write), it is a society on the road to extinction.

The Word and Reading-Writing on the Northern Border

1

In the area of the morphology of oral language, where oral language achieves content and signification, the word—from the simple to the complex—occupies the superior place. Then come morphemes, mor-phonemes, and lexemes (some linguists, wanting to simplify, stop the morphological chain right with lexemes, identifying these with words).

Without entering into current debates over the positivist charge of the morphological, I want to admit here to a consideration of the atomic elements of language—conceived thus as an organic system, a system of forms. In this I begin from the principle that messages form a phonic *continuum* without any more pauses than those necessary to take breath. In such a system, the word occupies a central place. In fact in it, one might well say, the system of links—or of atoms—concludes here. It closes here.

Taking the above as our foundation, we find that it is difficult to establish a universally valid definition of the word, more so even if this definition is inscribed in the terrain of the semantic or of the epistemological. Thus it is totally insufficient to speak of the word as the name with which things are designated or as a linguistic sign that expresses an idea. Equally insufficient are definitions such as the word is "an autonomous syntagm formed of inseparable monemes"[1] (Martinet), or the word is "that whole segment of a sentence limited by successive points in which no pause can be made"[2] (Hockett). In fact, then, until today all the efforts to give the term *word* an unquestionable objective validity fail in the face of all this lack of a proven fit.

But practice—particularly in terms of school grammar, that is, at the didactic level—has simplified things, establishing that the word is simply a form, an entity molded in a definite manner, capable of receiving as much or as little of the conceptual content of thought as the genius of the language permits[3] (Sapir). All and nothing at the same time? Given the above, linguistics in itself has preferred to remain at the lexemic level and to leave arguments over the word to rhetoricians, so that these can elaborate their lessons through them. The lessons, I might add, are stunningly brilliant, such as those of Ermilo Abreu Gómez,[4] who says that the word, once its origin has been identified, is the basis of prose and that which permits prose to be able to interpret the ineffable, to leap over the barrier of reason and to arrive at the miracle of expression. Later, Abreu reclaims the materiality of the word and says that literary language and everyday speech are really based in this dimension. Departing from the materiality of the word is what I am here proposing as the organic basis of an investigation into reading-writing on the northern border of Mexico, in the terms that follow.

2

To get research established in Mexico—in particular in the field of the social sciences—leads to serious questions about two matters that would seem to be very simple. One is to arrive at defining the problem with that simplicity of which Plato speaks.[5] That is, I want to know if my research problem really is pertinent and important. The other matter—and for me the more complex—is being able to offer a valid and creative response that departs in effect from the well-trodden paths and pushes out to the edge of moral validity (this moral validity is an ethical and not an epistemological problem in the strict sense).

The above two apparently simple premises have become the central core of the sketch offered here, which is nothing else than the basis on which in the near future (with years of study and experience behind it) we might construct a protocol of research into the teaching of reading-writing in the border zone between Mexico and the United States (in this case the city of Mexicali, Baja California, and the County of Imperial, California). That is, it is hoped that these ideas will be modulated into a project of solidly established research.

3

One of the key motives of these reflections turns on the open field[6] that currently exists in instruction in reading-writing and how one can investigate questions of a multiple nature that have repercussions, among others, in areas belonging to the theory of knowledge; the nature and function of communication and reading-writing itself; and, also, the nature and function of the school as a center for the reproduction of knowledge.[7] A second motive has to do with the specificity of the zone (example of a region) in which one must work: the Mexico-U.S. border (whose particularities are multiple and which moreover offers singular characteristics to broach the matter of investigation. In this case, we admit as an assumption that migration continues to be the basis and motor of the zone's population growth. Here a very rich market of tongues[8] has been created, This mix of dialects evades reduction to a unique and dominant model of speech and writing. Nevertheless, a paradigm exists—national language—which rejects the dialects and writings in all their variations that are manifest in this region.

Furthermore, we assume the interchange of cultures,[9] where—for social reasons of a multiple nature—the balance is tilted increasingly towards the predominance of the Hispanic (of the Mexican, even). This is already having an impact on the present system of education. To the degree that the Hispanic population in the U.S. grows, it daily confronts problems of a very diverse and complex nature in education.[10]

We close here with the observation that few investigations have been undertaken to analyze in depth the implications of the situations involved in planned research into reading-writing in our border context. In fact, current studies of the question have reported an object of analysis which remains vague and undefined.[11]

4

In the area of the reasons that have been established for conducting research, beyond the purely instrumental (which for me would have to do with tactical questions), there exists a more complex nucleus of ideas (Zemelman[12] speaks of levels of non-daily reality; Derrida[13] of the second level of discourse, where the opacity of reality is reality itself; Adorno[14] of the invalidity of the pure immanence of awareness). These support theoretical practice that seeks to concretize this research. Related questions are being passionately discussed in particular in linguistics and semiology, and also in psychopedagogy (without these ideas being inscribed in a unique and total way in any one of these areas of discourse).

In other words, research in turn wants to investigate its own pertinence, in terms of its role in forming the human individual. For a long time scholarly learning (or teaching-learning) has not put much emphasis on reading-writing or on developing reasoning abilities, to the detriment of more global and integrated processes of development of human capacities and skills.[15] (This is the reason, for example, that body language—just like visual and auditory languages—has in fact been forgotten, thus limiting the maturing of the infant, that is, limiting its capacities to communicate with others, with itself, and with nature).

Another area of relevance here is the highly polemical reasons given for instruction in reading-writing. Do the models come from the dominant dialectic and writing (Saussurean "language," in this case, the "national" language), or rather, as the proponents of the experiences of popular education[16] propose, do the models stem from the "speech" of the environment, which is to say, the *barrio*, the sector or social class to which the pupil belongs? This is a theme that cuts to the quick in the region, given precisely the existence of a such an ample market of dialects. In this connection, research would necessarily raise questions that imply confrontation between national and regional dialects; rural against urban modes of speaking and writing; or the social stratification of reading and writing. Connected closely enough with this is the issue of which technologies of reading and writing to teach: generic, everyday ones, or something more specific, which permits the learner to enter into relations with specific fields of knowledge (applied science, art, simulated languages)?[17]

Finally, one more related preoccupation turns on another polemical question in primary schooling in contemporary Mexico, the validity and pertinence of those methods used to teach reading-writing. The decree that tried to impose the global method as the "official" way is applied only partially. In fact, any empirical investigation would demonstrate that the generic model is found disadvantaged when confronted with the syllabic method and with onomatopoeia. By contrast, the global method would have to respond to questions that are increasingly taking shape. Before a growing iconization of the social processes of communication, the global method might not be the most adequate way to slow down a process that is leading individuals more and more to forget reading and writing.[18] How, finally, do we recuperate individuals' interest in these practices, subsumed as they are increasingly by the mass media of communication, especially television?

5

At this time, I would like to speak less about how to put the projected investigation into practice, but want to say only that once the problem is defined and delimited, given its nature, I am proposing involving the participation of diverse specialists. The object is to maintain from the beginning a multidisciplinary vision. Based on those methods and techniques utilized, we can thus guarantee the pertinence and validity of the information giving rise to reflection, analysis, and conclusions.

6

Among the reasons that have given rise to the practical implications of this study—beginning with the elaboration of a protocol—I would mention, specifically, two concerns for those generally interested as well as for those who eventually might be able to apply the results of the investigation, once it is concluded. Thus, the educational authorities of the state of Baja California are concerned with strengthening those processes that induce pupils (in general, all of them, but, in particular, primary pupils) to increase their interest by the practice of reading and writing in order through this means to strengthen their basic education. My other concern has to do with instruction in reading-writing in elementary school that feature bilingual programs, especially among those responsible for the different U.S. school districts along the border zone with Mexico (or those districts where high percentages of Hispanics are found).

In both cases, research results could meet such expectations as those linked to the pertinence and validity of the objectives and contents of plans and programs of instruction; design of pupils' skills and abilities profiles in order for them most effectively to be able to assimilate contents and objectives; validity of texts, teaching materials, and instructional methodologies; delineation of teachers' profiles, and a consideration of how their preparation might enable them to implement new proposals.[19] The above is inscribed in two perfectly defined concentric circles: the particular "school" context, and the "community" context (the social grouping and the historical moment in which this grouping operates). My hope is that this sketch will soon make it possible for us to arrive at the construction of a protocol of useful investigation into reading-writing methodologies as they are applied in our educational system.

Notes

[1]Jesús-Antonio Collado, *Fundamentos de lingüística general,* Madrid, Spain: Gredos, 1978, p. 212.

[2]Ibid.

[3]Ibid., pp. 213-14.

[4]Ermilo Abreu Gómez, *Arte y misterio de la prosa castellana,* Mexico City: Oasis, 1969, p. 23.

[5]In the *Georgias* and the *Carmides* the importance of the question is mentioned various times—that it be clear, simple, well formulated—as the basis of the method that originated with Socrates and gives support to Greek philosophy. Plato, *Dialogues,* Mexico City UNAM, 1922.

[6]Emilia Ferreiro, *Los hijos del analfabetismo,* Mexico, City: Siglo XXI, 1989, pp. 9-15.

[7]In this connection, there is an extensive bibliography, which it would be pointless to cite here. Rather, I feel it is necessary to continue the debate over the theme: is school today the best means to transmit knowledge? which school are we speaking of?

[8]Ferruccio Rossi Landi, *El lenguaje como trabajo y como mercado.* Caracas, Venezuela: Monte Avila, 1970.

[9]I refer to my essay "Chicanismo: esbozos para formular una teoría," *El oficio,* Mexicali, Baja California (1987), 61-8, published in this book as "*Chicanismo:* Outline of a Theory," pp. 69-78.

[10]A very complete panorama of problems and perspectives is offered in the works of various authors contained in *Oportunidades educativas*

y de investigación en la frontera, Calexico, California: Institute of Border Studies, 1985.

[11]The catalogue published by the Secretariat of Public Education (SEP) in Mexico (1988) reports only investigations that take into account the region as one more case. None of the studies reported there has to do, it seems, with the problem of reading-writing in this zone, nor does a first bibliographical compilation carried out in specialized libraries reveal significant studies for the case of the USA. The theme is only tangentially broached in J. A. Bustamente's *Uso del idioma español e identidad nacional.* Tijuana: Cefnomex, 1982 (mimeo).

[12]Hugo Zemelman, *Conocimiento y sujetos sociales.* Mexico City: Colmex, 1987.

[13]Jacques Derrida, *La estructura, el signo y el juego en el discurso de las ciencias humanas,* Barcelona, Spain: Anagrama, 1972.

[14]Theodor Adorno, *Sobre la metacrítica de la teoría del conocimiento,* Caracas, Venezuela: Monte Avila, 1970.

[15]Ferruccio Rossi Landi; Edward T. Hall, *La dimensión oculta,* Mexico City: Siglo XXI, 1983; Morton Davis, *La comunicación no verbal,* Madrid, Spain: Alianza, 1982.

[16]Laboratorio Educativo, "Lenguaje y cultura popular," in *Cuadernos de Educación,* No. 47 (1977) (Venezuela).

[17]Emilia Ferreiro, p. 143.

[18]At base, what is discussed is how to stop the retrogressive and "dumbing down" effects of the mass media of information, effects which, until now, have not been able to be reduced by instruction in and the pertinence of reading-writing such as they are currently practiced.

[19]Here I would mention the solid work done by Margarita Gómez Palacio, which has not found favorable conditions to be put into practice (her proposals have been published in different books by SEP in Mexico). Also of note is the work by Emilia Ferreiro already cited.

"... What Is Language, Anyway?"

One of the keys of all creative thought, in addition to its originality, lies in its capacity to offer new challenges to itself and to the thought of others. Dialectics is said to be an essential principle and reason for being of the processes that investigate all that unsettles and moves human beings—those creatures in context—there, in the world—of whom the existentialists spoke so emphatically, overwhelmed by the miseries of wars and post-wars.

It is certainly possible to produce this dialectical thought in the classroom, particularly if the teacher, with his skill and knowledge, establishes a real channel of communication with the students. But contemporary schools, bearing the current crisis of institutional validity, in reality show themselves little interested in this kind of thought, with which—without necessarily going back to peripeteia—it is linked very closely in friendship and the kind of informal talk that dialectics causes. I was able to get to know Lian Karp as a teaching colleague and friend, and always, in both facets, the strength of his creative thought and of his rigorous dialectical thought was patent.

The following notes testify not only to the feeling I have professed for Karp since I met him, but more than anything else they make reference to a theme we both discussed more than once, considering that he is a territory untouched by the traditional and ruling thought of our time—this thought which Lian, with his lucidity, was accustomed to reducing to the absurd. This is the case because, among other reasons, powerful themes and projects exist today that, by the mere fact of being broached, critique those paradigms that sustain, for example, the social sciences, and they put them in doubt.

Thus, Karp in his most recent writings—those that only partially gather what we covered in conversation—took culture as the basis of his reflections and broached, among others, the study of Gramsci, Foucault, and Habermas, in order thereby to elaborate his own ideas in the always unfulfilled ambition of all thinkers to continue circling about (perhaps like Parmenides) the idea not of a closed universe but of an always unfinished one, one always more charged with questions than with certainties.

When Karp spoke of culture he began with the essentials which, little by little, he would divide up—in the manner of a fine Swiss watchmaker—until he came upon the multiple articulations implicit therein. In the process of reconstruction, in the case of culture as Lian saw it, there appeared as a general frame of reference more than one closed and finished *construct*, a process he continually modified, in the same rhythm as history itself. Yes, for Karp the essential idea had to do with the existence of this Gramscian conception of hegemonic culture and subaltern cultures which—in society and above all in the interior of history—on interacting generate identities and differences. This general scheme then opened broad fields of reflection on the cultural, where a theme was located which Lian particularly preferred: how regionalism with its particular logic was inserted inside culture. Karp understood regionalism not as a synonym of chauvinism but as a profound vector of historical dynamization.

In the terms established by Karp, broaching the logic of regional cultures today of necessity highlights key themes that speak, among other things, of the crisis of the nation-state and finally of the ideological values emanating therefrom (here, in passing, one should recall Lian's preoccupations concerning ideology and the manner in which it goes on eroding individual and collective awareness). We are not speaking here of making a simple recension of a process that reality has smashed to bits, to the degree that modernity—the world initiated with the first industrial revolution—culminates its cycle of splendor in the 1980s and opens onto the profound and accelerating contradictions of the end of the century (some call this period postmodernity). To overcome simplicities and the obvious, social analysis would have to be simultaneously researcher and proposition, in terms primarily of weakening the nucleus of contradictions implicit in the cultural whole, in order, thread by thread, to see the real nature of this totalizing nexus.

A really complex task, Lian approached it from what could be called its deep roots, which are none other than those hidden in the daily life of peoples and are expressed in the nomenclature of the city streets, as in the elaboration and/or survival of customs and traditions, or, in a much more articulated manner, in local literary production, normally misunderstood and vilified by the metropolises. These cities are propelled to the death by a centralism and courting fashion in turn. They base part of their hegemony on maintaining the unbalance between conquered lands—the *provinces*—and that space which is the seat of central power.

Territoriality does not escape Lian's analysis. On the contrary, he places emphasis on the close correlations that exist between human societies and the environment and how the specific traits of regional cultures are generated through them.

To vindicate the regional through culture is not thereby reduced to being only a task of anthropological and literary recuperation; Karp's greater reason—which we find in his most recent writings—has a relevant historical meaning that, when well assimilated, leads to a confrontation with the reason for being of the conjuncture of social relations that bear on the increasingly feebler nation-states of our times. Above all, they suggest expectations about the predictable future—sometimes discouraging—of these gradually more decadent and obsolete realities.

If the present is not only the pure past, in its essence it carries with it indelible traits of the preterit, thus confirming a mediated historical mass by multiple elements as much of time as of space. In this complete scheme of relations and presuppositions, Karp's theses advance, causing us to see that in fact since the last century just like the nation-state national culture is a fallacy, or if you like a powerful ideological instrument to subject, in the interior of society and history, broad sectors of society—those in the provinces, for example—to the hegemonic ideas of national development. Suspicion leads us to ask: why are liberals, finally, using in Mexico the consolidation of the nation-state and its correlate, national culture? Led by fate, or on purpose? Is, in fact, regional culture not only a subaltern culture but moreover, in its trend of liberal encyclopedism, a "poor" and obsolete culture? Is this really *popular culture* or the entire culture of the provinces?

Next step. Culture is not only a process but also a product of the palimpsest type, of various and diverse readings, which are not always found visible by everyone or located there on the surface. And it is here—I return to Karp's ideas—where the investigation becomes particularly fruitful if one admits that the real culture of the regions is a relegated culture, little known and spread—naturally!—by hegemonic culture. That is, the real cultural function—that which is initiated with agricultural production, *with the work that makes the ground produce,* and ends up being thereby a *physical culture* and a *spiritual culture*—is maintained continually in force as a daily practice of all social sectors. Through this practice subaltern cultures consume essential parts of their identity, usually confronting and evading simultaneously the nomus (order) of the hegemonic culture, the *power* of which Foucault speaks. It is here, in this continual confrontation and evasion, where common sense opposes "science;" where metalanguage—*albur,** for example—preserves tradition; where a street name recalls the originary topology of the city and its daily history; and, finally, where the street poet performs his daily task—a little the Homeric task or that of a true priest of knowledge—of giving faith, from a clandestine vision but not therefore any less valid, of the incessant unfolding of true popular culture.

We finish eating spaghetti, emptying our glasses of red wine, then begin our coffee and go on talking with master and friend Lian Karp—my feeling for him is vast—about everything and nothing at the same time, "because," as he suddenly asks, "what is language, anyway?"

---

*A picaresque statement with a double meaning.

National Symbols:
Their Impact on the Border

Frame of Reference

Part of an investigation that has been begun, the notes that are here presented develop a series of hypotheses (in the case of the social sciences it is increasingly difficult and useless to speak of isolated hypotheses), which want to clarify processes through which the individual is inserted into his or her immediate reality. In this way, what is being attempted goes fundamentally to the heart of things; it does not depart at all from empirical results but rests on and elaborates theses obtained through the reading of different authors. Suppositions and hypotheses are forwarded that result from experience that has been produced in the field of the theory of knowledge and as a result of analysis and study of the theme that through time has come to be called national culture. Above all, it attempts to systematize the result of continued, lengthy treatment, sustained by many other critics and colleagues, dedicated always to attending to Mexican children, with whom the exchange of experiences and opinions has been continual and enlightening. All the above is today bathed in this special experience which represents daily life on the northern border of the country. Taken as a whole, what the writing seeks is to justify the beginning of an investigation: *for those Mexican and Mexican-American children who pursue their primary and basic education in Mexico and in the United States, how is the presence of what here is defined as "Mexican national culture" made manifest?*

Just as with all the investigative processes of which they form a part, these notes have as their objective arriving at a delineation of a series of aspects that today appear widespread in pragmatic questions like the elaboration of textbooks, the treatment of the child in primary school, bilingual education, resistance to the processes of cultural assimilation, and, finally, how culture is interrelated with a social formation so complex as that of the existence, in different territories, of similar populations, whose cultural origins are the same or similar. Their results could eventually serve as criteria to redefine or consolidate practice.

In this way, what I am initiating attempts to be part of the group of contributions that today seek to define with the greatest precision possible the problems implicit in the analysis and comprehension of the identity of the culture of a people so markedly heterogeneous as the present-day Mexican, and by extension the Mexican American. In a more formal way, these notes would play the role of frame of reference for the process of investigation mentioned.

It is a frame of reference that is restricted to certain plans of an ideological character and which does not even assume, at the level of the design of hypotheses, questions such as social stratification and awareness or territorial location and incidence of determining factors. Emphasizing the analysis of the national within the country's territorial arena, the discussion seeks thereby to interest also those beyond the northern border to defend with particular decision and certainty their cultural origins, and all that implies in the economic and political spheres. I am referring, of course, to the Chicano population of the United States.

The National Symbol

Usually, in the analysis of the national symbol[1] (understood here as the originary and founding essence of the concept of the "national"), the historical perspective leads back, on the horizon of time, to the epochs in which the "nation-state" emerged, that is, to the epochs in which territorial and cultural heterogeneity was subjected to the economic and political interests of that social class which, to confirm its hegemony, required geographic borders and common ideological elements, both defined with absolute precision. Thus, the nation encompassed different peoples within a territory and imposed a group of common values and symbols on those who inhabited this territory. Necessary to consolidate the social advance of the bourgeoisie as a class, these processes—the territorial and the ideological—would later influence in a diverse way the historical development of the nations.

In fact, the national symbol would be consubstantial in appearance with the origin of the nation without regional borders and with common ideological values. In Mexico, as is known, this historical moment is registered in the middle of the last century, after the loss of half of the national territory, and when the liberals promoted the institutionalization of certain common national symbols: the anthem, the flag, language, laws, identity (that which speaks of the "Mexican" as a natural essence unmediated by other cultural essences). This was so even though, in fact, the nation-state promoted the patriotic symbol, which is identified with state institutions and not the national symbol, which would be that identified with the origin of man and his first settlements.

That is, the antecedents of national symbols cannot be reduced to so narrow a sphere of time. Its origins, as effects of this work, are inscribed in a much broader perspective, which is linked with the origins of the human being and the way in which these origins are conceived by primitive peoples.[2] Thus, to understand the function of the national symbol one must then lay out its origins. These origins explain the function of the symbol and, for example, its source within the diverse sectors of the population. It is a complex and still little-studied source mediated by ideological problems of class.

In this way, the national symbolic encounters its explanation not only in the immediate relation which is established between the individual and the nation, but in the deep necessity of the individual to utilize a certain type of "safety belts" which make his most immediate universe comprehensible and habitable. In the first case, the national symbol would be synonymous with the patriotic symbol. In the second, the national symbol would be linked more with the cultural essences of a people (language, territory, myths and customs, and social organization for work). Thus, the symbol is always, in its origins, expression of a myth;[3] that is, it always expresses a process of substitution of realities. Hence, in the origins of all national symbols—understood as cultural essences—there will always be found very remote antecedents that speak basically of the reification of the individual (a process by means of which man is "confused" with that which he is not, generally because he neither understands nor dominates "this other").

In this way we then think of the origins of our national symbols. *Our national symbols* (which will here be called patriotic), and not only those that promote the state, but in general those that promote social institutions, and that also incorporate the essence of the national. In this way, the national would be not only the patriotic, and would emerge and be consolidated in a parallel manner with the nation-state, but, in general, that which founds and gives reason for being to a people and changes it into a specific society. In the case of this country, an essential characteristic of the national symbol is to have sustained itself against the most diverse processes of cultural amalgamation (syncretism) that the country has suffered. The deepest and most acute of these is Spanish-indigenous mixing.

Without attempting an exhaustive analysis of all the national symbols, I do want to analyze some of what I consider the most outstanding, sometimes not the best known. Thus, in the catalogue of these symbols, for analytical purposes the maternal figure, the idea of death, corn, the flag, and the anthem occupy a primordial place. It is worth stating in advance that as is seen not all these symbols have a direct relation with school education today, given that its link with the patriotic is tenuous. In addition, it does not deny its national origin, to the degree that these are essences that the majority of the population share. The implication of this will be seen further on.

Hence, we begin with the maternal figure, which appears in all human cultures. In the origin of the maternal figure, social organization first would seem to be the causal root of this symbol: the human would identify in the mother a natural source of protection when faced with the environment, which would lead to divinizing whoever offers this protection. In this way, in the majority of the theogonies a good part of the gods are represented by feminine figures, which in the form of the mother and female companion have different names. This feminine, specifically maternal figure is present in the theogonies of the country's indigenous peoples and receives names like Coyolxauqui or Tonantzin. She is a figure that then, in the Conquest—one of whose least studied facets is the form in which cultural syncretism was channeled—is transformed by the dominant ideology into the virgin Mary (Juan Diego and his *ayate**), to achieve, one way among various, the evangelization of the indigenous peoples, with the goal of thus subjecting them more easily to the designs of the conquerors. To explain the Catholicism of the Mexican people is to understand, among other things, the survival, in religious symbols (the maternal figure among them), of the oldest and deepest traditions and customs of the pre-Hispanic peoples. In this way, it is to understand the type of sympathetic relation which ecosystems as complex as those that predominated throughout the national territory give rise to. Immersed therein, man established multiple and complex relations with nature to guarantee the survival of both. Thus, the maternal figure, insofar is it is a symbol, here encounters its source: in nature, in the earth.

The idea of death is also a symbol that has accompanied us Mexicans for years. Its actuality has never been lost. As with the maternal figure, death is also a symbol consubstantial with the most ancient human beings (the best studies of the myth and its function clarify for us precisely that it is around death that the deepest psychological motivations of the human being revolve). In our case, as much the indigenous as the Spaniards venerated it. Moreover, one should point out a strange singularity in this symbol for Mexicans: the "disrespectful" way with which our people, different from others, confront not the entire idea of death and its significance, but a part of it. This irreverence is what gives substance to the symbol for us. Death makes Mexicans laugh, cracks us up. In some way, it is the companion who always accompanies us. I mean, we Mexicans say, "Why sweat it, if we're all going to kick anyway?"

Corn, as a food base, similarly has a notable presence in our culture, and therefore it also symbolizes the Mexican in more than one way. Think, for example, of the *tortilla, tamales,* or *pozole,* foods that have to do with the being of the nation (understood in the broad sense). In turn, corn generates about it a whole series of activities—the cultivation, consumption, and transformation of grain—which causes us to think that Mexican society integrates an entire group of deeply rooted cultural practices around corn, establishing this food as one of the most precise and clearest national symbols.

Patriotic symbols in their current representation, the flag and the anthem are nothing less than the continuity of the banner, standards, and hymns of war characteristic of the "flowery wars" of our peoples. Banners, standards, and hymns that Hidalgo's hosts brandished and sung on throwing themselves into the fight for independence were sanctified and became a sign of the *chinacos*** confronted with the French. They became native guide and song during the Revolution.

That is, in each national symbol we shall find remote origins and in these their deep source among the peoples. Doubtless, this explains the fact that their study and veneration in school should never be neglected.

The persistence and depth of the national symbol goes a long way toward explaining the existence and influence of certain cultural tendencies promoted in particular through the mass media of communication, which erode community: the mythification and mystifying of mothers, kinship (the *compadre*), the social hero, and the family.

National Symbol: School and Family

As was just said, not all the national symbols are the object of school study and knowledge (at least not in all public schools). In one way or another in the schools, the national is seen as linked with the patriotic, since article 3 of the Constitution has already established this connection. This is clearly one of the most valuable and relevant contributions of liberalism: a liberalism that has been identified as the initial promoter of the nation-state and that saw in the strengthening of the national consciousness a way to reduce and limit the alienating control of the church in those times when social contradictions were different from today.

It is not odd, then, that it was Valentín Gómez Farías himself who in Mexico was charged with propounding and supporting what was already then known as civic education in the public schools of that time. This was nothing other than the systematic and organized study of national symbols. I return to insist anew on the national symbols of a patriotic character, since public education in Mexico continues to be a product of liberalism. As such, public education does not include in terms either of study or of veneration any national symbols that are partially identified with religion (the maternal image) or the popular (the idea of death).

In this way, education has been changed into a vehicle for indoctrinating especially the child with those principles and norms that plug him into the nation-state. Moreover, it is not only the study of civics in school which permits the student to link up ideas of the nation, national identity, and national culture. Paired with the above, a series of rituals are practiced in other social institutions that affirm the value of the national in the child's mind.

For now, overlook the effect or effects of the situation just described and first consider at least two things. First, how is the relation between school and family founded (when I refer to school, I always have primary school in mind)? In the second place, how does the study of national symbols extend or limit children's fields of knowledge?

With regard to school-family relations, one should take into consideration that these—perhaps without seeking either in the family or the school—are contradictory today. The socializing function of both institutions is counterposed at least in what is referred to as the transmission and apprehension of national symbols, as much of cultural as of patriotic origin. Thus, for example, while in the family the most deeply rooted traditions and customs establish the preservation of certain national symbols that lay education forgets, on privileging the diffusion of other national symbols (the flag, respect for institutions, national heroes, laws, and norms) school would seem to oppose, in daily experience, the socializing tendencies of the family, given that the spread of these symbols on the part of the school does not recognize the source which the maternal figure and the idea of death have in the consciousness of the majority of the nation's individuals—that is, in the family as institution. It is difficult to understand if, for example, the fact that if the maternal figure is linked with religion, it is sufficient for the school not to take into account this national symbol, or whether it shouldn't attempt to explain with greater rigor and objectivity the idea of death and the founding role that this concept has among the nationals. A way of recuperating a better relation between school and family (a relation that here is thought to be deteriorated) would be to study, and to promote in both, the national symbols, *all national symbols,* and the amalgamating function that they have from the social point of view.

Today school and family are also contradictory, in the area of national symbols, because of the loss of value that the patriotic symbols register (to those that are linked with the government), and that are exalted in school, while in the family circle they are degraded and minimized. These are clear effects of the contemporary economic crisis.

To have an idea of the contradiction described above, an attentive, detailed reading of the free civics textbooks in primary schools would suffice. In these textbooks the national is circumscribed and reduced to the study and preservation of the most restricted notions (patriotic symbols, the origin of laws and institutions, human rights), in place of attempting a broader and deeper analysis in this respect. And the above in no way is free, if we take into consideration the simplest study of popular culture (that is, that which is linked in terms of customs and traditions with the majority of the nation); we would see the subsistence since remote times of *all* national symbols and their transmission through the generations. Let's take as an example the population in the marginalized urban zones of the great metropolises. In this population there lives on the deeply rooted idea of death, a profound and untrammeled respect for the maternal figure, and also, clearly, the cult of the patriotic symbols such as the national flag and coat of arms. Other, more *ad hoc* examples would be the case of "race," that is, the Chicano population that lives in the United States, which vindicates with its most refined values the Virgin of Guadalupe (nothing else than the Tonantzin of the Aztecs and which is also, at the same time, the maternal figure), to the *pachuco* (who bares his teeth at death), *tortillas,* and Villa and Zapata, both invested with the strongest, most rooted patriotism. These examples could be multiplied even further.

But in another sense, the promotion of the national symbols through educational processes has another significance, related in a strict sense with the processes of knowledge. How is the national symbol related to the processes of knowledge? To answer this question suggests one of the most consuming problems in the area of epistemology today. As a source of deep disagreements, polemics, slippery areas in which one should necessarily step with caution given that it is rowing against the current, to speak of how education promotes national symbols always implies making suppositions and hypotheses, speaking against ideological tendencies that have been around for more than twenty centuries.

To relate national symbols and processes of knowledge, I want to propose a gradual but deep change in the way that man in general, the child in particular, is put in contact with his environment. Obsessed by the necessities implicit in the principle that to count and to measure are the central ways through which man relates to his environment, we might forget that this way of working out contact with the world reduces and schematizes the processes of knowledge. It limits and inhibits other human faculties that also permit man, in the same way, to know his world, his environment; a world and an environment that are not limited either by mathematics or by logic but which also contain elements that can be apprehended more easily by the imagination and fantasy. This would imply, therefore, the utilization of the different disciplines of knowledge, as well as the existence of realities (objects, subjects, languages) not limited by reason. In fact, insofar as knowledge advanced by the hard and inflexible ways of counting and measuring, the man's capacity to know was restricted. The object of knowledge was substantially reduced.

One should ask teachers and colleagues who develop their professional activities in constant relation with the processes of teaching-learning—and here is found one of the keys of this study—how much of the knowledge we impart or of the methodologies we utilize are found to be disconnected from formal languages, from stochastic methods or probabilistic functions. Isn't "science" by chance continually looking to relate and confuse the subject and the object, causing the former to appropriate the totality of the latter, carrying to an extreme degree the reification of the subject? The tendencies that I will call neopositivist, and which are those that predominate in the area of the theory of knowledge, cause their effects to be felt at all levels. Therefore they found and sustain the theories of education and learning at the primary level. This means, among other things, that teaching and learning in primary school are increasingly leading into the areas of rationalism at all costs and empiricism to the letter of the law, implying as well that the areas of knowledge that have the most to do with learning and the appropriation of national symbols are gradually losing ground faced with so-called scientific knowledge. Myth, for example, they say is not "true," from which it follows that all knowledge founded on myth has no validity. Therefore, indigenous people's deep knowledge of plants and homeopathy has no validity, nor do the taxonomy and processes of sympathy that primitive man established with nature, as well as the knowledge of the social and psychological implicit in primitive religions. In many ways, this accounts for the origin and reason for being of the national symbols and the motive of rejection and ignorance on all levels of study in primary school.[5] Each day the child more imperfectly knows the patriotic symbols that emanate from the nation-state, and he tends almost totally to ignore those symbols which are also national which we have claimed have a cultural source. These symbols are related to and located in a more regional, local environment, that of the neighborhood and the community.

I would like to leave these remarks as one more preoccupation among others, one born from experience. What is suggested here is a hypothesis. I would like these comments to interest people as a source of concern born of experience which I feel will soon, unfortunately, be validated by facts.

National Culture and Mass Culture

But the above are not the only areas in which the national symbol is presented as an object of polemics. If only. Today other areas exist where a profound fight is being fought between the national symbol and currents against it, and without doubt these areas are closer to us. I refer to the struggle taking place between national culture and mass culture.[6]

Without doubt we can more clearly locate the importance that the promotion and study of the national symbol has in this area, placing emphasis on it since the early years of education. As mentioned above, both the school and the family are the two particular institutions charged with promoting an awareness of the national in the child. That is, it is through them that the child forms his idea of national culture, *his* culture. Culture is essentially composed of the following elements (which are changed into symbols at the same time through different processes): territory, language, myths and traditions, and social organization for work. In both cases, then,—as much in the case of school as in that of the family—mass culture concretized in the messages that the mass media of communication transmit assaults and tries to make national culture disappear through sometimes subliminally, sometimes openly imposing values and customs that are not those of the nation, nor do they promote the formation of a more integrated, more capable human being, one more capable of relating with his kind and his environment.

At this point the contradiction is unresolvable. While in one way or another the function of the mass media of communication is not regulated, the formative task of the family and school will be continually sabotaged. The disadvantage of the family and the school when faced with mass culture is increasingly obvious. Not coincidentally, mass culture's attack on the family and the school is directed particularly towards the formation of awareness that supposes the channeling of the national symbols in the individual, as has been well demonstrated in recent studies of the issue:[7] it is easier for the primary-school child to identify television personalities than national heroes. They know more about the word "duck" (and of the image it carries) than about the flag and its respective image.

Moreover, it is not only the child who suffers the brunt of mass culture. Recent studies[8] have also demonstrated that the primary teacher dedicates a substantial part of his free time to television and that he knows more about current soap operas than the pedagogical theories of Rafael Ramírez or Jean Piaget.

In another sense, we should be cautious when treating the problem of national culture and its link with mass culture. Instead of developing the argument here, I only want to indicate that in the case of our country national culture stems from a culture emanating from a national whole: *mestizaje,* which gives origin to a specific culture and identity:[9] Mexican culture and identity that are not purely indigenous nor purely Spanish. In the Mexican, in the culture implicit therein, there are mixed and syncretized elements of indigenous cultures and of a Spanish culture that previously was seen to be made up of a multiple mixing of cultures: the Celtic and Gaelic, the Latin (and finally the Greek), and the Arab and Moorish. This culture, deriving from multiple sources, is that of our people. The majority of the Mexicans are *mestizo.* Therefore, we have in our origins very diverse symbols that nourish our nationality (symbols that the processes of synchrony numerically unify and reduce). This accounts for our deep nationality, not that exhausted in the chauvinist or the patriotic. Such a culture is undoubtedly the base of our artistic and folkloric wealth.

But the existence of a dominant national culture does not suppose, or at least should not suppose, the gradual disappearance of the aboriginal indigenous cultures and peoples of the country. These cultures and peoples in ways of which we are both aware and unaware are now suffering the brunt of present-day proposals for modernization, which do not respect their most refined values, origin and sustenance frequently of our deepest national symbols. Cultures of the neighborhood in the strictest sense, the indigenous cultures therefore are the target of mass culture (universalizing and homogenizing), which directs the best forces to distort and ridicule indigenous, autochthonous cultures.

Without doubt, a task that primary school in particular should undertake is to promote the stubborn and deep defense of neighborhood cultures, that is, indigenous cultures, in the teeth of mass culture's sustained and brutal attack. Perhaps in some such defense the survival of education itself is at stake.

National Symbol and the Border

There are many and different ways of beginning the study of our country's northern border. Here on the border, phenomena of a growing complexity are processed. Perhaps because of this the area is attractive. In this way, the research proposed here would seek an explanation for some of these phenomena. I am going to suggest some questions that exemplify where our uneasiness in this regard is leading. These questions sustain the investigation being suggested.

What are the possibilities of harmonizing the peoples whom the border now divides? Is some kind of union possible? Is it desirable? How would this union function? What are the barriers? Will by chance the process that now keep populations of common origin separate be irreversible, populations which blend in the same culture, whose national symbols are equal, similar, or identical? What can be hoped for in this regard?

In the eagerness to give answers to these questions, I do not want to play the role of soothsayer but only to find tan explanation for the social dynamic, an explanation emerging from suppositions elaborated up to this point.

In this way, I want to insist on a principle: that of culture, that is, the amalgamation of territory, language, custom, traditions, and social organization of a people. Thus, in the case of the Mexicans as a people, our national culture is not subject to the past century. This isn't its historical horizon. National culture in the case of Mexico—as understood here—is extended a bit more in time and congeals to the degree that *mestizaje* has advanced; that is, to the degree that the Spanish and the indigenous have changed into a single essence, losing their original characteristics.[10] To admit the above it would be necessary to recognize which territory corresponds to this culture, which language, which traditions, which social organization. I believe we all know the answer and know that in spite of Santa Anna national culture does not have actual borders, in terms of territory, for example.

Moreover, we would have to ask—in the same way in which the indigenous and the Spanish are mixed—if there hasn't occurred a similar process of amalgamation between the Mexican and the "North American" in the northern territories of the border which originally were Mexican; or if each of these cultures shares territory alone and not the rest of the component elements of culture. I shall venture one more hypothesis: in fact North American culture is a "weak" culture, made of several mixes, whose bases are the central and northern European cultures that do not offer resistance, as history demonstrated, on displacing the "strong" cultures (those that, like the Italian, for example, and also the African cultures, have purer ethnic origins). Given the above, my hypothesis would therefore include the supposition of the inevitability of the predominance of the "strong" Mexican culture over the "weak" Anglo Saxon culture, particularly in those territories which on some occasion were Mexican. The above, in fact, would cast down theories that speak *in terror* of the predominance of the Anglo over the Chicano, and that see in the country's northern border a territory already won by the culture of the "barbarians of the north."

The above on the one hand. On the other, following also the supposition of the predominance of "strong" culture, I would suggest the hypothesis that lacking a solid culture, the Anglo Saxon population in particular would tend to make itself the "strong" culture, especially in the border zone, by having been Anglo Saxon territories on one occasion. These territories were themselves of the "strong" culture and territories, moreover, in which the population of Mexican origin, gradually predominating, would tend to become more permeable to Mexican national culture.

In the above considerations, I make an abstraction of a process: the fight between mass culture and national culture, trying to adjust between this "frame of reference" and the structure of this argument. In addition, I recognize, in terms of culture, that this fight implies the principle contradiction. In the tactical, the strategic, I maintain my thesis: the chief contradiction in the sphere of northern border culture is seen in the struggle between "weak" culture and "strong" culture and in the cultural origins of the territory. Continuing with the development of this thesis, I would then like to amplify my hypothesis in terms of the importance which is accorded, in the long run (implying in the short run the realization of urgent and enormous tasks), the promotion and strengthening of the national symbols—particularly those of a cultural source—between the populations of both sides of the border. Also I want to stress the strategic role that work with primary-school children (and elementary school on the other side) can have, if we take into consideration how it is that at this school level the transmission of knowledge is determining. In addition, as was said, there is an attempt to promote qualitative changes in the processes of knowledge themselves.

National culture, border culture, and school culture would thus be indissolubly linked.

---

*apron

**guerrilla fighters

Notes

[1]"According to Peirce, that sign in which the sign-object relations designates its object independently of the similarity or identity with the object or of the relations with the object. It only depends on the interpretant, which elects a medium for the designation of the object, and which then ceases in the communicative process in a conventional manner (according to some laws). The symbol, which does not reproduce its object, nor signal it directly, designates a type of object, not an individual object. The object designated by means of a symbol is always general. All simple signs (for example, words in a dictionary) are, with respect to their object, symbols." Max Bense and Elisabeth Walter, eds, *La semiótica,* Barcelona: Anagrama, 1975.

[2]In appearance, in whatever ethno-anthropological study it is possible to find information in this regard. But, here it is considered that studies like those of Mauss, Lévi-Strauss, Eliade, and Canetti are less "contaminated" by ideological detours that make difficult the comprehension of the phenomenon in the terms being suggested here.

[3]Bense and Walter.

[4]Exemplified here, only through Piaget: the "scientistic," that is, neopositivist bad habits of genetic epistemology. And one should not forget, in this regard, the weight that Piagetian theories still have today in contemporary didactics, in particular in processes linked to reading-writing or the formation of the numerical symbol in pupils of primary-school grades.

[5]The basic problem, here, is how, for example, in a project that contemplates a basic education of ten grades, to incorporate a new education, an "other" education, removed from the paradigms linked to "scientific rationality" and which recuperates, for example, what Ernest Bloch establishes in *Sujeto y objeto,* or the suggestions of Korsch, Marcuse, and Adorno.

[6]Mario Margulis perhaps has the greatest precision in broaching this problematic, showing those basic characteristics of the contradiction which are established between popular culture and mass culture. For now, let's leave to the side entering into a discussion of mass culture, as conceived by Margulis, as in effect a *culture.*

[7]Among others, see the works of Cremoux, Alvarez Manilla, and Bernal Sahagún.

[8]Ibid.

[9]The polyvalence that the concept "culture" has acquired causes confusion. One of the most common misunderstandings confounds culture and society. This confusion produces problems of definition in regard to national identity. In the case of this study, national identity is a product that society and not culture generates.

[10]To broaden this conception, see my essay titled "Indigenismo y colonialismo interno," in *Crítica,* No. 20 (October 1984) (Mexico, City, UAP), 18-24.

References

Adorno, Theodor. *Consignas.* Buenos Aires: Amorrortu, 1973.

Aguilar Camín, H., et al, eds. *En torno a la cultural nacional.* Mexico City: INI-SEP, 1967.

Benjamin, Walter. *Iluminaciones / I.* Madrid: Taurus, 1971.

Bense, Max, and E. Walther. *La semiótica.* Barcelona: Anagrama, 1975.

Bilbao, Elena, and María Antonieta Gallart. *Los chicanos.* Mexico City: Nueva Imagen, 1983.

Bloch, Ernst. *Sujeto y objeto.* Mexico City: Fondo de Cultura Económica,1983.

Canetti, Elías. *Masa y poder.* Barcelona: Muchnik, 1982.

Esteinou, Javier. *Hacia la primavera del espíritu nacional.* Mexico City: Programa Cultural de las Fronteras, 1989.

González Salazar, Roque, ed. *La frontera del norte.* Mexico City: El Colegio de México, 1981.

Hostie, Raymond. *Del mito a la naturaleza.* Buenos Aires: Amorrortu, 1968.

Ivanov, V. V., et al. *Los sistemas de signos.* Madrid: Comunicación, 1972.

Kahn, J. S., ed. *El concepto de cultura.* Barcelona: Anagrama, 1975.

Kristeva, Julia. *Semiótica y praxis.* Barcelona: A. Redondo, 1973.

Marcuse, Herbert. *Ética de la revolución*. Madrid: Taurus, 1970.

Merani, Alberto. *Naturaleza humana y educación*. Mexico City: Grijalbo, 1972.

Piaget, Jean. *Naturaleza y métodos de la epistemología*. Buenos Aires: Proteo, 1975.

Resnikov. *Semiótica y teoría del conocimiento*. Madrid: Comunicación, 1970.

Shardakov, N. M. *Desarrollo del pensamiento escolar*. Mexico City: Grijalbo, 1968.

Silín, Pedro. "Del fetichismo de las audiencias masivas de la educación para la comunicación." *Intríngulis* 3. Mexicali, B.C.: 1991, 23-32.

Suchodolski, Bogdan. *Tratado de pedagogía*. Barcelona: Península, 1970.

Verón, E., et al. *El proceso ideológico*. Buenos Aires: Tiempo Contemporáneo, 1967.

Chicanismo: Outline of a Theory

Introduction

Every day the affirmation is becoming more of a commonplace that the crisis now affecting Mexico has served not only to reveal but also to accelerate certain social problems. With the crisis, the contradictions in all senses that face a society like ours have been made more transparent and evident. Day by day new and more acute social contradictions are appearing, which goes to show that this solid and stable edifice which Mexico had seemed to be from the war (the era of stabilizing development) to the governments of the crisis (say, from 1975 to the present), no longer is as much. On the contrary, Mexico is a building that shows fissures, whose cracks threaten to cause the walls to collapse. Entire spaces will be revealed and changed into a no man's land, into power vacuums that will have to be occupied. Although there are still many actors on the scene, the struggle doesn't seem to be going in anyone's favor.

But perhaps we are dealing with something that is not so noticeable or evident that the deep contradictions—whether territorial, political, economic, or ideological—now affecting the country will not remain here, in this country. Of course, one does not speak of the obvious, of that which is the plain truth, namely, the interrelation and interdependence between Mexico and Central America. What happens, for example, in Guatemala, Nicaragua, or El Salvador generally has a profound influence on Mexico. Reference is made rather to questions less obvious, less evident today, questions that have to do, doubtless, with the daily life of the United States—like it or not, the United States. Once again I want to stress that I am not referring to the most immediate, that which by being located most directly at the economic base impacts in the most explosive—although perhaps not the most important—way the relation between Mexico and the United States: the acute implicit and explicit problematic represented by the case of undocumented workers and now the Free Trade Agreement. Again what I am here referring to is a situation that, since the last century, has been alive, expectant, unresolved. This is clearly a problem with a complex solution: the Chicano population, their relation with Mexico, their being in and of itself, their expectations. What is their uncertain future? What is our relation—as a country and as individuals—to them?

Thus, what I want to suggest in these brief notes is a sketch, from the point of view of a Mexican analyst, of what could be a perspective on this situation. As some of us Mexicans see it, from this side of the line, our relation with Mexican Americans may have a common future. My emphasis in what follows will be to understand this possible future as developed through a discussion of several ethno-anthropological or cultural questions.

The Chicano Problematic

What does history allow us to see in this respect? In general, the inclination of history towards economy is a secret to no one: the former finds in the latter—rightly so—the most certain explanation of its project. But in this process one commonly forgets that daily life, the material of history, is not only economic, and that to understand it in its real dimension one must also look into its political and ideological aspects. That is, one would here speak of a cultural vision of daily life, as that vision which integrates (or at least attempts to) all the elements that conjoin to give social facts their concretion and reality.

In this way—and consider the precarious, synthetic, and occasionally schematic quality of these notes as the result of the restrictions of space—one might affirm, in principle, that the analysis of *chicanismo*, just like what follows with other themes, generally registers the existence of interpretations inclined towards the economic, which has given rise to a partial or rather an incomplete view of the phenomenon. At least little emphasis has been put on the interrelation that eventually could be established between Chicanos and Mexicans—the viability of this interrelation. If said interrelation is not possible, why not, in cultural terms (instead of only in economic, political, or ideological)?

In this way, history, just like all the history of the region, reminds us that with the territorial division of the last century a large part of the Mexican population stayed anchored in the areas annexed by the United States. But what kind of population was that which stayed behind on the other side of the line?

We recognize, for example, that this population was noticeably stratified from the social point of view and that hence neither its economic, political, or ideological situation was held in common. This is something that most discussions of the theme pass over. Thus, for example, at one extreme of the stratifying scale one might locate the ranchers, for whom integration into the new society was less traumatic, since they already were able to alleviate the impact of the annexation with their economic power. At the same time, their customs had more from the Spanish than from the *mestizos* or the indigenous (and don't forget that in fact *mestizaje* in Mexico was considerably consolidated in the era extending from post-independence to the Reform). Therefore, between ranchers and ranch peasants—extreme opposites in our stratification—there existed the unresolvable contradictions from the cultural point of view (the most totalizing). In fact these contradictions marked the existence of different and differentiated populations, which from that time comprised the nucleus of the Mexican Americans. To forget this matrix has lead to idealizing the indigenous as unique root of the Chicano: Aztlán as the promised land, that is, not only the original land, but also a utopia where all social contradictions will be resolved through this principle that supposedly will unify all, taking as its unique or primordial basis the indigenous. In present-day Mexico, the thesis of the existence of a homogeneous national culture sustained by the indigenous (what indigenous? the peoples of the Central Mesa; the complex cultures of the south—Chiapas, Yucatan; the hunters and gatherers of the desert?) is sharply questioned. It is increasingly displaced by a pluricultural vision of phenomena, in which the definition of *mestizo* continues to be the heart of the problem.

There is another analytical view of the problem (of which I shall limit myself to the basics that have stood out the most). Tightly linked with the economic, this view establishes the continuity of migratory flows and bases the permanence and depth of Mexican culture in the U.S. on the existence on these flows. Unfortunately, this view does not establish with any precision just what this "Mexican" is. We never learn how these flows occur in terms of permanence and depth, that is, how much the Mexican-origin population remains in place once it has managed to cross the border. Nor do we see how it influences and has influenced the cultural questions (economic, political, and ideological) of the Mexican American population already definitively settled in North American territory.

One might speak of a third current, one beyond all theorization and incapable of it. Bluntly put, this view suggests the full incorporation of the migrant into his new society, dissolving in this process of incorporation all his ancient cultural baggage. Thus, at the same time that he is stripped of his mother tongue the individual forgets even his own name and together with it all his previous cultural trappings (work sometimes strips away his physical traits). Lacking the capacity to theorize, this current—totally subordinated to the dominant capitalist ideology that predominates in both the U.S. and Mexico—is daily gaining ground and threatens to overwhelm the other currents. In particular it is encouraged by the mass media of communication on both sides of the border.

Chicanos: Economy and Society

The problem of economics stems not so much from performing an analysis of the forces of production. Rather, this problem minimizes the interrelation of the factors that influence and determine the meaning of history, passing over the complexity of diachrony and inserting social analysis in conjunctural questions—pure strategy—without taking into account the truly strategic and overvaluing the empirical as expressed through an excessive formalism. In this way, we want to establish a critique of the economism that until now has partially veiled the study of the phenomenon. But at the same time my discussion focuses on unmasking the over-ideologization of the problem. This over-determination of ideology suggests aspects linked to ethno-anthropology in their corresponding historical matrix as a basic and central source of *chicanismo.*

What does this mean? Although these observations are hurried and schematic, I want to say that in its core my argument emphasizes at least two questions. One is related to the economic, and the other is related to the ethno-anthropological, although both are connected by a common theoretical conception: historical materialism. (For the moment I leave to the side problems of definition of the term *chicanismo*).

In this way, an economic perspective acknowledges that the Chicano as individual is not alone but that he is in society—in North American society in the first instance and then in its connection (whether or not sought out) with Mexican society. As such, he is equally stratified along with the rest of the population. Thus, his essential interests vary according to the place he occupies within the social formation. Similarly, this economic situation or position is the determining factor that influences at the moment of establishing relations as much with the population of undocumented Mexicans (the majority of them poor farmers, although the population of marginal urban origin is rapidly growing) as with the Mexican population that seeks to open up relations of a political character with the Chicanos. This latter population is located in the government and political parties or organizations of opposition.

Factors also of importance and necessary to consider when one wants to analyze the Chicano situation are the processes of industrial reconversion of the current phase of capitalist recycling (the installation on the west coast of the United States of the point industries of this country; the proliferation of in-bond twin plants on the northern Mexican border; an agriculture increasingly linked to the U.S. market, among others) and the conservatism that today permeates North American society. These factors both bear on the determination of the population flows of undocumented Mexicans who go to the U.S. and on the relocation or change of work status of Chicanos.

In fact, I want to found the central part of this work on a theory of the economic: to design some suggestions for the reconstruction of a theory that explains the ethno-anthropological substratum of *chicanismo*.

From Economy to Culture

At the beginning of these notes, I spoke of the necessity, in terms of social analysis, of "de-economizing" this analysis, attempting to inscribe the political and the ideological in a cultural perspective, within which the economic is balanced. I wanted the interrelation of factors to be established, each properly defined. To the degree that this has *not* occurred with the problematic of *chicanismo*, it is valid to make new, different suggestions. These, then, start from the "de-economization" of the analysis more broadly and deeply bearing on the political and the ideological. In this case, I have attempted to make suggestions about the ideological, starting from the supposition that it is in the areas of this ideological where the ethno-anthropological problematic is located.

Thus, I would like to establish some principles or categories in order to be able to take as a basis the assumption of a relation between Chicano and Mexican. This relation occurs on many levels, ethno-anthropology (or more generally the cultural) being one of the most outstanding. In this way, culture is the central category in this part of the exposition. My main hypothesis in the field of ethno-anthropology will be elaborated around culture.

By culture I understand a society's or people's conjunction of material and spiritual goods. These goods are grouped in four great concentrations: territory, language, myths and beliefs, and social organization for work. Linking culture and people in the case of Mexico, this connection implies the existence of a pluricultural society whose dominant characteristic is the origination of a *mestizo* sector of the population during the Conquest, which now dominates over the indigenous sectors (more or less 10 million people, grouped in about 50 ethnicities). Although Mexico has its origins in the sixteenth century, as a defined pluricultural society it is not until the beginnings of the nineteenth century that a nascent capitalism offers citizenship papers to the *mestizo* as differentiated cultural component. Thus originates syncretized, specifically Mexican territory, language, myths and beliefs, and social organization for work. Dominant in Mexican pluriculturality, *mestizo* culture is the result of the mix that occurs between the Spanish and the indigenous, where the former openly dominates the latter. As such, Mexican *mestizo* culture is of a marked Greco-Latin origin (supposing that the Greco-Latin was imposed on the Arab, the Celtic, or the Galician, among its other cultural sources).

In this way, Mexican *mestizo* culture dominates the entire scene of the country until the middle of the nineteenth century, when it breaks up (it is thus seen to be physically limited) as the national territory is split, although in these territorial spaces that are lost the Mexican-origin population resists, forgetting its cultural origins (those apart from the territorial). This occurs as much because they are deep-rooted to them, as because, in fact, never until today has the flow of Mexican population stopped towards these lost territories. Hence the subjecting through syncretization of the Mexican to the Anglo and the Saxon by a process that has never been completed. Based on the above argument, we can see how it would be difficult for such a process to reach fruition. Moreover, the cultural *grows* more rapidly than the demographic in the territories annexed during the nineteenth century. In the correlation between population and culture, the second grows more rapidly, which explains the survival and rooting of Mexican cultural traditions among the Chicanos.

Within the scheme one fact stands out. If Mexican *mestizo* culture is diachronically subjected to the Spanish, on the level of synchrony the indigenous is solidly rooted and survives, in force, in the cultural whole which is the *mestizo*. Hence, the Chicano understands his cultural source in the indigenous present in the *mestizo*. But doubts might occur on this score. Today the Mexican *mestizo* in effect has indigenous dominance. In the last analysis, perhaps in this respect it's worth more to establish that the recuperation of the indigenous on the part of the Chicano fits with the category "culture of resistance," which a people vindicates when it looks for its liberation or confronts the culture of its conquerors. In the Chicano "culture of resistance"—a *process* more than a *product*—would thus fit the indigenous, the social rebel of the end of the nineteenth century (Joaquín Murrieta), the popular hero of the Revolution (Flores Magón, Villa, Zapata), and the "pachuco" and the "barrio" (more for what these last represent of the marginalized, thereby rather confronting the dominant culture of the U.S. than, as Octavio Paz asserts, identifying with other essences of Mexican culture and identity).

Only some (not all) Chicanos would identify themselves as defenders of this "culture of resistance." This leads us to recognize not only stratification as such but also the definition of the strata. In this way we can spot a future mutual agenda in terms of class between the populations of both countries (Chicanos and Mexicans). Such a task requires a specific analysis. Only thus can the idea be forwarded of assimilating as rough synonyms the terms "race," "Chicano," and "vato," applying these terms to those who offer cultural resistance to the mass culture of the society of consumption and negating whatever pejorative meaning these words might have.

A second moment in this scheme, which calls above all for the development of the historical in other regions of the world, would include the assumption of the inevitability of the predominance of "strong" Mexican culture (with all its *mestizaje,* and taking into consideration its Greco-Latin origin) over "weak" Anglo Saxon culture, particularly in those territories that were once Mexican. The above counterbalances those theories that speak fearfully of the predominance of the Anglo over the Mexican and that see in the northern border of the country a territory already won over by the culture of the "barbarians of the north." Similarly, following the supposition of the predominance of "strong" culture, one might suggest the hypothesis that lacking a solid culture, the Anglo Saxon population in particular would tend to make the "strong" culture its own, especially in the border zone, by having once been the territory itself of this culture. Moreover, because the Mexican-origin population in this territory has gradually predominated, it makes itself more permeable to Mexican culture.

But also we should consider cultural syncretism in at least two senses. First, such mixing occurs in terms of the principal contradiction referring to culture in the region. We note a hegemonic culture (mass culture) generated by the society of consumption and the village cultures—emerging, marginalized, subjected. Second, consider the fact that, in their eagerness for mutual self-protection, village cultures have established bonds of kinship and union among themselves, on the margin of their ethno-anthropological origins. Thus, it is easier for the Chicano to link himself culturally with the original inhabitants of these regions or with the emigrant from other countries than with the robotized Anglo Saxon man of the North

American cities (the example is extreme, but it offers ample possibilities).

The Political As Conclusion

In fact, we cannot negate the connection between the Chicano and the Mexican. This will be more fully manifested to the degree that capitalism digs in. An unavoidable characteristic of this process is the *de-hegemonizing* of the cultural, to the degree that capitalist culture, that is, mass culture generated by the mass media of communication and the patterns of consumption, assaults village cultures, the emergent cultures, or those of minorities (for example, think of the amendment on the use of English in California or in the operation of the discriminatory Simpson-Rodino law). Such cultures are almost obliged to enter upon a process of self-defense, of self-consolidation. In this sense the bonds between Chicanos and Mexicans need to be strengthened. Beyond the economic, this includes an analysis of the cultural as a process of exchange of experiences in the area of theoretical analyses whose conclusion touches on at least the following four points:

a) Are Chicanos and Mexicans different peoples?

b) Based on the response given to the above question, what type of relations should be established between Chicanos and Mexicans?

c) Faced with the development of specific societies, what is the future of both peoples?

d) In the precise historical framework that contemporary North American society represents, how does stratification among Chicanos work?

Constructing Regional Cultures

Proposal

In those contradictions driving the Mexican social structure, relations established between periphery and center, usually favoring the latter, have been especially dynamic. If anything has characterized this country, it is its marked *centralism.* In the course of things, such a force opposes the *federalism* that should characterize our socioeconomic formation.

Stemming from the economic, centralism affects the whole of the functions and relations that occur between the periphery and the center. It respects neither space, nor does it manifest apparent limits. Its effects, thus, are shown to be devastating in more than one way. In the cultural sphere, the effects of centralization substantially inhibit the development of the regions and restrict manifestations of the multiple artistic expressions, and culture in general, which have their seat and origin in the periphery. Given the above, centralism presents itself as one of the most significant obstacles to cultural development in the regions, the communities, the villages, and among the ethnic and social minorities.

Therefore, something needs to be done in this regard if one wants to contribute to cultural decentralization, to achieve a state in which artistic expressions developed here respond to the needs of our environment, to support the creative contributions of local artists. Taking the above as a basis, we feel that the resources which the official organisms assign for cultural activities should be channeled through applications that guarantee effectiveness in cultural and artistic promotion.

Fine. How is this to be achieved?

Introduction

For some time in Mexico, there has been a steady drive to establish a series of criteria that define the concept of national culture, at least since the period of the Reform. Ramírez and Altamirano, for example, broached theories in this regard. Of course it is not by chance that this need receives special expression starting in the middle of the last century. During this period, our history registers spasmodic movements of society away from feudalism (among other things, its ideas of territory and dominion) and is pulled by the dynamic of the new mode of production. For development at the level of the socio-economic formation, capitalism requires a nation-state. That is, apparently erected on top of social classes, a State is needed that submits the ensemble of social sectors to its dynamic and to the dynamic of society which corresponds to it.[1] This is a long and difficult process, which even today continues in force inside the recurrent crises. It is a process, in the end, that dominates in the economic, the political, and the ideological.

Within this process the urge to define national culture has been maintained as a constant. What are its components and its ways of functioning? What are its products? The vicissitudes in this respect have been diverse, but all have closely corresponded to the dominant ideological conception that feeds the revolutionary project with its roots in nineteenth-century liberalism. This project has to do with the encyclopedism of the French Revolution, Comtian positivism, and, to a lesser extent, anarcho-syndicalism. This latter has persisted until the present. when the ideological project of the State and of the dominant class is nourished by very diverse contributions, with the object of thus complying with one of its basic functions: to be the escape valve for social conflicts and theoretical support of economic and political action of this class and of its State. It is no coincidence that technocracy, scientistic neopositivism, and developmental theories such as internal colonialism all share in this project in order to preserve equilibrium in the system, thereby achieving the objectives it proposes.

In this framework, national culture has indubitably followed the dynamic that characterizes the economic process, the dominant of all social processes. Thus, the most basic characteristic traits of national culture are its marked centralism; its subjection to consumption and fashion; its tendency to be urban rather than rural; its corruption of leisure time (in particular, that of the working class, although not only theirs); its imposition of the consumption of vain and alienating products; and the privilege it shows toward intellectual over physical work. In such a scheme, what can regional cultures hope for? What are they? How are they made up? Is it worth the trouble to construct or reconstruct them?

Culture? What Is It?

One commonly hears acknowledgment of the term culture's polyvalence. I don't want to summarize why this polyvalence exists even today, generating much debate, but rather I would like to go beyond it to set the rules of the game. That is, I shall offer my own understanding of the term culture, somewhat removed from howwe have understood it. (However, I freely acknowledge as antecedents Taylor and Morgan, White and Lévi-Strauss, and, above all, Marx and Engels.)

Thus, for the purposes of this study culture is the conjunction of material and spiritual goods proper to a society. These goods fall into four great concentrations: territory, language, myths and beliefs (including art), and social organization for work (including art). The above is called cultural structure, which in turn gives rise to a series of functions. On operating, these functions generate products. In some such terms, we can see that the confusion which accompanies the use of the concept culture has much to do with the confusion that occurs between cultural structure, function, and products.

Now then, as with all human products, cultural structure, its functions, and its products are not immutable. In its entirety, everything is subjected to the dynamic of social change. To the degree that society changes, culture changes, and between both there is a close interrelationship mediated by work. Neither human society nor culture can be properly understood except as a function of work. A society and its corresponding culture change to the degree that the processes of work become more or less complex. These work processes determine the social as well as the cultural structure.

Thus, to explain culture one must explain society in the context of the work that gives rise to it. Today, for example, three great spheres refer inevitably to the social. The first is the mode of production. By imposing rules and principles of work (of the accumulation of capital) at the world level, the mode of production corresponds to the existence of a culture at the world level that stops feeling its effects on the rest of the "cultures." The second sphere of social and cultural existence is the socioeconomic formation, subordinated, to a different degree, to the dominant mode of production. "National culture" corresponds to this second sphere. Finally, the third sphere is the forms of production (whose social and territorial impacts often do not go beyond the community or the village). Here a group of "subcultures" is found (without this term having a pejorative meaning): regional cultures, those of social and ethnic minorities.

In fact, *as structure,* one can speak of the existence of a universal culture only as capitalism, because then socially and technically cultural functions and products acquire universal validity and therefore offer vast territory to culture to manifest itself.[2] These functions and products, on the other hand, speak of and explain a process of domination (or one of the phases of this process), which seeks to break the life of the village by imposing the universal community's values. Such values are sustained, for example, by the apology of violence, with consumption as the way to gain access to well-being, the mercantilization of daily life, and the incorporation of technology and knowledge of productive processes.

Faced with this dominant structure, the cultural structures on the national level are hotly debated and attempt to overcome their limitations. The most acute of them gives solidity and permanence to the domination of the bourgeoisie as a class. Development and survival of regional and sectorial cultures are limited or annihilated, be they ethnic or not—that is, those social groups whose conduct by nature opposes the order that underlies the dominant social system. Neither the indigenous, women, homosexuals, nor national minorities have real and effective voice and vote in the majority of the social and cultural structures at the national level. The validity and existence of these cultures is intimately linked to the dynamic itself of the class struggle.

"Universal" Culture

The integration of "national" culture is manifest as a process through continuous confrontation which occurs between foreign influences upon originary culture and the forces of this latter to resist these influences. This process is initiated at the moment in which society, as part of the economic and political dynamic, is obliged to subject the states that populate a territory to some form of unity. In terms of political economy (which epistemologically are those that give greater clarity in this respect), this happens with the passing from feudalism to capitalism.

In the case of Mexico, it is only at the middle of the nineteenth century that this process of defeudalization begins to manifest itself. Moreover, this happens in the context of Conquest and Colonialization and so of necessity is shaped by the economic and political values implicit in their ideological principles, which have the force of "religion." The function and character of ideology during feudalism are explained through the political and economic power that the Catholic Church accumulated during this period. In Mexico it is not during feudalism that the structures of "pueblos" that had existed during the pre-Hispanic epoch are broken. Nor did the *encomienda* or the Vice Regency destroy those cultural structures proper to the indigenous peoples of the country before the Conquest. The socioeconomic dynamic of feudalism is found in the subsistence of these cultures—no matter how physically exploited they may have been. This gradual process of destruction of indigenous culture is initiated in the middle of the nineteenth century. Together with the physical destruction of individuals and the depredation of their natural resources—which was consubstantial with the Conquest and Colonialization—indigenous languages, customs, and traditions are systematically destroyed in order to pave the way to *mestizaje*.

Ideological defeudalization, and therefore the construction of a culture that was at the same time "national" and "universal" and that would correspond to the new social conditions, is guaranteed by the adoption of a group of alienating ideas that during the last century had "France" as their most obvious source. These ideas of the Enlightenment, of liberalism, and of positivism impelled the ideology of the Reform and of the Revolution at the beginning of the century. Today, particularly through the pernicious influence felt through the mass media of communication, there exists something amorphous but enslaving identified as "the American way of life," whose negative characteristics have already been mentioned: consumerism, subjection of fashion, loss of the individual, and metropolitanism.

Never has there been a peaceful relationship between the "national and the "universal," only a continual contradiction. Underlying the entire process of definition of "national" culture, we find the problem of which form this should take to assimilate the values proper to "universal" culture. These values in one way or another express high points of the human achievement. The dominant culture requires assimilation, wanting to validate and to obtain recognition from "national" culture.

One of the most contradictory currents of culture is rooted in all this. Seeking to reconcile civilization and primitivism, this current has tended to disqualify aboriginal cultures as inoperative and primitive. In fact, these latter in their essence and in reality deny the modernity which dynamizes the conceptual content of civilization. Indigenous cultures in particular are subjected and eliminated in honor of civilization. Such a civilization, identified with "universal culture," is not a cultural structure (no society, at any moment of its being, has generated pure civilization or pure barbarism) but, at the most an ensemble of cultural products, usually artistic, that the members of a given society have created individually or collectively. The undeniable universal validity of these products is not sufficient to give rise to the notion of cultural structure.[3] Civilization, thus, is only a *product* (a group of products) and not a *structure*.

Expressed in the spheres of both the national and of the regional, civilization transcends territoriality and is inscribed in the most deeply valid of the human processes of knowing, of gaining access to reality, and of dividing up and distributing social work in intellectual and physical terms. In fact, all "civilizing" processes (whether of the Spaniards during the Conquest and Colonialization, the Gallicization of the positivists and liberals, or Televisa through the mass media) seek the destruction of regional and minority cultures, requiring their conformity to the single model that this process imposes: a supposed "national" culture that, always in the name of civilization or modernity, denies validity to the aboriginal cultures that pre-existed the always forced nation-state.

To summarize, in one way or another "national" and regional cultures are saturated in this complex of contradictions which generates the assimilation and integration of "universal culture" and the false disjunction implicit between civilization and barbarism, which parallel how physical and intellectual work are seen in class societies. Conceived in this framework alone, pluriculturality, which could impel the support of regional cultures, should be analyzed.

"National" Culture

Within the above scheme, "national" culture, from its initial establishment at the middle of the last century, has sought the essence of an identity: *the Mexican.* The essences accumulated in "national" culture have to do fundamentally with the myths, traditions, and customs identified primarily with pre-Hispanic and even more so with Mesoamerican cultures. Thus, death, birth, rites of sexual initiation, and the maternal figure are some of the basic ingredients tossed in at the moment one tries to cook up Mexican identity, and in this way "national" culture. In a certain measure, therefore, "national" culture has had to be an entelechy, an abstraction, the metaphysical skeleton of an ideological process that has remained blind to the whole of social relations. More than culture, in some ways national *society* becomes a *raison d'être* for the establishment of *the Mexican.*

In another sense, apart from its link with identity, "national" culture has also had to become a concept that attempts to subject to a unifying principle what on the regional level is conceived as a variant of the national. That is, the national is not an essence but a group of essences, amalgamated, of course, into something amorphous and undefinable, without it mattering that these essences are contrary and opposed to one another in different ways. Now that the different indigenous cultures are not called *mestiza* (mixed)—not to mention the different mixed cultures themselves—what can unite indigenous and mixed cultures at a given point in time? What identity is there between a Huasteco and a Yucateco, between the native inhabitant of the Federal District and the inhabitant born and living in Morelia (not to mention Baja California or Sonora)?

If our theory cannot deny the existence of a *national society* (conceived in terms of *mestizaje* and the inhabitants of a geographic territory identified as the republic), this in no way means that the form is one and indivisible in which this culture functionally operates and generates products. An operative level of this culture at the regional level and of social strata in which the interrelations established among the elements that comprise it in some way add fuel to the emergence of singular functions and products at the regional level or at that of social space. Thus, it is possible to speak of regional languages, regional ways of being, myths and customs proper to a region or a social stratum. It could be, in effect, that the incidence of pre-Hispanic culture is a factor that exercises predominance, but in no way is it the only one. Without doubt, however, its value and dominance are explained in historical terms because the manifest tendencies of all processes of cultural definition seek origins. In the case of our country, these roots have much to do with indigenous cultures (the same does not happen, for example, in the case of the United States, where the aborigines and their cultures were razed, violently erased from the map).

In addition, regional culture is not a problem centered in the opposition between non-indigenous and indigenous cultures. Its definition advances more complexly. As I will try to show later, there are other factors, apart from the indigenous, which operate at the moment of establishing a definition.

"National" Culture and Regional Culture

In effect, no one can deny, at a given moment, the amalgamating function of this diffuse "national" culture, principle and basis of *mestizaje* in more than one sense. It is a basic element to unify the will of the nation. Carlos Monsivais says that in this country the Virgin of Guadalupe and the national flag are capable of mobilizing almost the whole of the population (they already have). (This is even more the case if we are talking of confronting the gringos, for example.) One should not forget, however, that the Virgin as well as the flag syncretically summarize the diversity that confronts Mexico as a people. In the *Guadalupana* the indigenous root is clear. In the flag this same diversity exists. Have we by chance forgotten the pennant of Hidalgo and his men? In other senses, however, this "national" culture does not erase differences, at least in two aspects: class and region. Even though we are here addressing the latter, clearly in the case of the former national values are not the same for rich and poor. Thus, the nation will never be egalitarian, nor will it be able to erase any of these differences. Most of the time, a cultural structure of national character is understood only as sum of cultural structures, a sum that does not unify but that should respect and promote differences.

In the regional, the nation should not conceive itself as that which unifies and erases differences but as that which respects and promotes the cultural vocations of the country's different social groups. From the ethnic point of view in Mexico, these are many peoples from throughout the territory.

Before explaining what I understand by "cultural vocation," I'll offer several counter-examples. Think of what has been the linguistic policy of the country until now. In reality, in Mexico we can speak of the existence of a multitude of languages (many of them unwritten). *A fortiori*, these languages are being driven under in honor of a Spanish that, not even in its own origins, was unitary (what we call Spanish here resembles the Castilian language in Spain). What's the point, then, of imposing a language, instead of preserving the mother tongue? Precise dates in this respect do not exist, but, at least in the case of the indigenous population, it is alarming the way that the number of speakers of aboriginal languages is decreasing, and the aboriginal languages themselves. Before the arrival of the Spaniards there were more than 700 languages and dialects in existence. The problem of language is complicated if, in addition to Spanish, the Chamula and Pai-Pai are forced to learn to dance the *jarabe tapatío*. What remains, for example, in the case of Ensenada, of that special life which developed at the beginning of the century, the sustenance of a highly enlightened urban center? What remains of dance in Veracruz or of religious practices in Morelia? Tepito continues to be Tepito where the neighborhood was a social nucleus of particular solidity and security. In fact, in its eagerness for modernity, the "national" destroys, terminates all that physically and spiritually opposes it. I don't know if it's already too late; today one can hardly speak of Mexico as a pluricultural country. But what is this? How should it be understood?

Cultural Vocation

In the case of Baja California, for example, the basic characteristics that would permit speaking of the existence of a regional culture are, among others, the following: the predominance of ecosystems dominated by the desert, to a lesser degree by the sea (Ensenada) and the river (Mexicali); the existence of an aboriginal indigenous population, formed by hunting and gathering peoples, who today confront acute processes of extinction; a diffuse colonial past framed in the missionary action of the church; and periods of uprooting and territorial anarchy, which furthered the presence of North American adventurers in the countryside and the cities. Given its character as a border territory, Baja California is a geographic space marked by a broad ensemble of relations of interdependence. And with a population fed by massive migration, Baja California is syncretic and diverse, its residents originally from Michoacan, Oaxaca, the Federal District, or Guanajuato. Syncretism and diversity explain, in part, the emergence of urban subcultures—*cholos*—who reclaim a place, their *place,* in the social whole, breaking the *nomos,* the order, which they do not understand but which they know as rapacious and unfair.

Just as one can identify strong cultural traits in Baja California, so can one for many other regions of the country. This regional diversity, on occasions clearly dominated by the indigenous, is what enables us to speak of pluriculturality.

In this way, the cultural vocation which founds a regional culture should explain, recuperate, and put into functioning (recycle) that which has made conservation of a given region possible. How long does Chiapas have left for its jungle, and how long for the life of its indigenous groups? How much longer will the sidewalk *cafés* of Veracruz last, and the *danzón** and all that it signifies? What chances for survival does bigotry have in Morelia? Aren't they looking to conquer the desert in Baja California and thus destroy all the culture it generates?

Respect for cultural vocation is seen in several spheres. The broadest comprises the so-called ecosystems, the base in which is inscribed a non-predatory relation between man and nature, that is, mutual respect in terms of survival.

The second sphere of reference is historical. Following Horkheimer, we understand the content of cultural monuments as conditioned by the history of the tensions and oppositions between social classes. For example, the liberty suggested by Greek statues is twofold: liberty to lead a heroic life represented by the symmetry and beautiful naturalness of the Greek statues showing adolescents; and liberty of being safe from oppressive work and misery. The missionary work of the Jesuits in Baja California or the splendid Enlightenment of Ensenada cannot be otherwise understood. It is impossible to comprehend the products without referring to the dynamic of these oppositions.

Finally, the third sphere of reference is ideology, which essentially reveals the opposition between life and death, the many ways in which man has confronted this opposition. Here, we are on terrain where art, religion, and myth are interlinked to construct culture through respect for cultural vocation. This recognizes that man, indistinctly, can and should develop physical as well as intellectual work. All can simultaneously be productive workers and artists, and with the same rights. Everyone, therefore, should have this opportunity. Art, myth, and religion are nothing more than different ways of distracting death, vicariously playing its role. In this game, everyone has something to offer.

Although this discussion has been brief, it remains only to conclude saying that now the challenge is for Baja California and its inhabitants, as well as for the different regions of the country and their inhabitants, to know if it will be able to respect, and to make respected, its cultural vocation.

---

*typical dance of Veracruz

Notes

[1]In different works Marx develops this idea in its full scope and implications.

[2]The universalization of cultural functions and products is explained through the mechanisms by means of which imperialism operates: international division of labor, armament and militarization, concentration and centralization of capital, accelerated and totalizing mercantilization of daily life.

[3]This universal validity is determined by the development of capitalism as mode of production. Only through it can cultural functions and products, whether or not artistic, achieve this universal validity, itself explained only in terms of the market.

References

Aguilar Camín, Héctor, ed. *En torno a la cultura nacional.* Mexico City: INI-SEP, 1976.

Engels, Friedrich. *Dialéctica de la naturaleza.* Mexico City: Grijalbo, 1961.

Horkheimer, Max. *Sociedad en transición: estudios de filosofía social.* Madrid, Spain: Península, 1976.

Hostie, Raymond. *Del mito a la naturaleza.* Buenos Aires, Argentina: Amorrortu, 1968.

Kahn, J. S., ed. *El concepto de cultura: textos fundamentales.* Barcelona, Spain: Anagrama, 1975.

Martínez, Pablo L. *Historia de Baja California.* Mexico City: Libros Mexicanos, 1956.

Marx, Karl. *Fundamentos de la crítica de la economía política.* Havana, Cuba: Editorial de Ciencias Sociales, 1970.

_____. *El capital.* Mexico City: Siglo XXI, 1975.

Piñera Ramírez, David, ed. *Panorama histórico de Baja California.* Mexicali, Baja California: UABC Press, 1983.

Folklore, Resistance, and the Border

—for Guillermo Gómez Peña
and Harry Polkinhorn

In the great night my heart will go
Darkness comes toward me rattling
In the great night my heart will go.

—Papago song by Juana Manwell

Introduction

Culture and folklore are two terms whose polyvalence characteristically limits and sometimes distorts analyses in which these terms play a central role. On occasion becoming ambiguous, this polyvalence causes themes touched on by the terms to take on a high degree of subjectivity, a rich impressionism. Moreover, when the theme "folklore and the border" is broached, one finds one's material for discussion all but vanishing.

Taking the above into account, the work I am presenting—very concise and concentrated owing to limitations of time and space—is almost altogether hypothetical. Indeed, what is not hypothetical in this material? Proposals, therefore, will be formulated whose objective is to enrich reflections that focus on the theme, as well as related empirical investigations.

Part of other research I am currently engaged in, this discussion is linked to these investigations and acknowledges in particular the sharing and exchanges of points of view which I have had with Alfredo Velasco, Rogelio Reyes, and Reynaldo Ayala. Their opinions have helped me much. But, clearly, what is claimed here is only my own responsibility. Ideas in formation, the following analysis hopes to be enriched with opinions, criticisms, and suggestions.

Human Group, Culture, and Folklore

In the precarious framework which an intervention of this nature represents—if time and the complexity of the theme are taken as indicators—it is necessary to define several concepts. Thus, my analysis begins by defining three concepts, through which I will unravel the cloth, let's say, singing this *corrido.*

The first of these is community, better yet, human group, such as Morgan[1] in particular understands it: various individuals who share in common the gregarious instinct. This also involves motives of defense and feeding or reproduction.

To all human groups a *culture* will correspond as consubstantial function, pretty much as Taylor (closely following Morgan) conceives it.[2] As function of the group, this culture is broken down into what has elsewhere[3] been called territory, language, myths, and social customs and organization of work.

In all culture originally—that is, before social division of work—folklore exists, understood as human action without destination, in the immediate present, towards survival and physical reproduction. Folklore in essence reflects the capacity of man, according to his innate interests, to tackle different forms of expression mediated only by the correlation that occurs in the individual himself between his material and his spiritual being (both being totally human and concrete); between the individual and his species; and between the individual and his natural context. These correlations express the presence of man—of the human, to be more precise—in culture.

To understand folklore *today* one must begin with these three conceptions and verify their historical development, that is, through time and work.[4] Here, we enter upon one of the most polemical points of this material: does folklore change or not? Is it unitary, or how is it constructed each time it emerges? If it is unitary, how does it reproduce itself?

Although I won't summarize how this polemic has recently been handled, I will say that I am especially indebted to Gramsci[5] in this respect. Thus, folklore is understood as the originary manifestation of culture in behavior and feeling, leaving to the side territory as pure matter but not the use to which it is put—of a people (of a human group). But if it is certain, says Gramsci, that folklore is unitary, its permanence is explained only through the fact that within the evolved human group—that is, no longer the first and originary—there is a generally broad sector that continues to use this folklore. This sector, adds Gramsci, whether or not numerically it is in the majority, has never been hegemonic in any society until now. Gramsci calls this sector the "popular" and invariably identifies folklore with popular culture, or those cultures that resist the hegemonic: emerging, subordinate cultures.

But how do we link the previous reflections to the concrete question of how folklore on the border is expressed? Does this folklore by chance exist?

Folklore and the Border

Here I shall focus basically on three hypotheses. In the first, the border is a historical concept, which has been in force between

Mexico and the U.S. approximately since the second half of the nineteenth century. Therefore, this historical division is not the root that permits us to locate the origin of one, or two, or many folklores on the border, given that the border dweller would thus be defined by accident more than by substance.[6] Similarly, in this line of reasoning I would also doubt those claims that the folkloric has to do purely with the Mexican (on both sides), or with a poorly defined hybrid Mexican North American.[7] No, I would go further—the second central hypothesis of this section—and would claim that folklore here has to do more than anything with the existence of an ecosystem dominated by the desert,[8] which has hosted a series of characteristic human groups. I am thinking chiefly of hunting and gathering peoples, opposed to sedentarism and farmers dependent on irrigation more than on rainfall. Therefore (as I hope to prove later) the folkloric roots of this region have to do with these peoples more than with Aztlán, as is generally admitted. In any case, Aztlán is only a paradigm of Mesoamerican cultures, confusing though it may be.

In my view, the third equally polemical hypothesis is concerned with a revision or rewriting of the Gramscian theses: if I admit as valid the existence of a unique and originary folklore and of its conservation and transmission through popular culture (which I insist is always a culture of resistance), I have shaped this conception and say that if popular culture on reproducing itself has folklore as its basis, the former continually recycles the latter to confront hegemonic culture through resistance. I shall now pass on to a demonstration of some of these claims.

Manifestations of Border Folklore

In the scant bibliography on this theme (on which work has hardly begun[9]), West's recently published book *Mexican-American Folklore*[10] exemplifies well enough the tendency which has dominated studies and investigations: "folklore: and "border" are regularly identified with the Mexican, or with the Mexican North American.

They leave out at least two equally valid cultural sources which sometimes have more presence than the source mentioned above. That is, on speaking of folklore and the border, we should not forget that in this region—understood in its broad sense—we find the culture of the Indian peoples who have lived here since ancient times. Also there is the singular and syncretic Anglo Saxon culture of North America.[11]

One should add another element. Significantly, the three cultural manifestations that occur in the region are unified—or at least tend to be—in that their uses and customs are somewhat similar. Which shouldn't seem strange; it would explain the two hypotheses being tested here. The first establishes which unique and common roots folkloric uses and customs have (understood among all human groups as action not destined in an immediate manner to survival and physical reproduction). The second delineates the correlations that mark the essence of the folkloric, in which the "individual-nature" correlation[12] occupies a noteworthy position.

Following West, I would note that in the region those uses and customs that stand out indistinctly in the case of the three cultural manifestations—Mexican, indigenous, and Anglo Saxon—are basically oral tradition, practices connected with the earth (also having to do with agricultural practices more than with habitation or transportation), feeding, graphic representation, carving of figures in stone and wood, and music. Empirical studies in this respect would permit a demonstration of the singularity achieved through these uses and customs, marking a radical difference between this region and others, whether the United States or Mexico.

From the Rural to the Urban

I would now like to consider how folklore tends to be a set of practices very similar in different regions, no matter how removed they may be geographically one from the others. Two reasons explain these similarities. First, migratory movements occurred years ago, explaining, for example, the population of America. Comparative studies in anthropology[13] point to great similarities among several central Asian and Mesoamerican cultures, including some from the humid tropics of America. The migration hypothesis helps to understand, in part, the similarities of folklore all over the world.

What better explains these similarities, however, is a neglected hypothesis, which holds that all these human activities of "artistic" distraction have their origin in the rural sector; they deal with rural life. They are linked with this natural context. Music "imitates" the sound of the wind or of birds. The oral tradition speaks of the deeds of the hunter or of the warrior. Dance "imitates" the steps of the deer. Painting appropriates the "spirit" of things (animals, plants, the elements). Into this unity, each people introduces differences, matrices, singularities.

What meaning does the above have for the border? One implication has already been indicated, the identity that exists between folkloric practices of the three border cultures. Another is how they have mixed, blending the folklore practices of the border especially with those of the center of the country, with those of the Mesoamerican indigenous peoples and those from the humid tropics: the celebrations of the Mixtecs in Tijuana or of the Michoacans in California.

Another especially complex problem concretizes the relation, and simultaneously the rupture, between folklore and city. Here reflection advances slowly. The complexity of the theme is immense, and doubts and uncertainties accumulate that generate "new" folklores. But are they really new? What can be called urban folklore? Thus, for some authors,[14] with the emergence of the cities simultaneously marking the hegemony of the rational over the magical and the religious, folklore stops as such and is transformed into "art" as one more result of the synchronic process (something that *goes on being,* in essence, that which it *is*), of a diachronic phenomenon. This process socially limits the "artistic" within society. "Art" corresponds to the elites, "folklore" to the masses, even though the expressive, "aesthetic" quality of folkloric products is often equal to or better than that of artistic products.

Along the present-day border, how many of the manifestations that we would call "new urban folklore" have an evident link with the originary, with the rural? Doesn't the "graffiti" of the *cholos* cause many to recall the rock paintings of other times? Perhaps the motorcycle and the pick-up truck recycle the horse? Doesn't the *corrido* keep alive the oral tradition? In this regard one could cite many another example.

Folklore, Border, and Resistance

To conclude, I want to underscore several ideas about how border folklore resists the encroachments of the culture of global society, called mass culture.[15] All kinds of culture are resisted, which is becoming a particularly significant experience in this region. If indeed to talk of folklore already implies resistance in itself (the rural confronting the urban, the popular the hegemonic, the Indian resisting his disappearance), today a process is emerging which confronts modernity in order to overcome it. Consciously and unconsciously, this confrontation has connections with the folkloric, but not in a reformist way (apologizing for nationalism). Rather, the process arrives at folklore because only as such is it thought to be important. I speak here of an aspect of postmodernity, which in its most relevant practices is constructing a common front with the folkloric.

That is, this region is being pressed from both sides of the border by a pathogenic centralism as much as by hegemonizing and discriminatory artistic practices. Hence, artists and intellectuals are beginning to construct a discourse of creation and reflection[16] that establishes in its most relevant premises resistance not only to centralism but also to its consequences, offering an alternative practice that questions the source of the dominant practices. Among other premises of their discourse, this alternative practice is distinguished from and so is related to folklore by envisioning the totality of language as means of communication; opening spaces to the iconic; justifying limited territory as generating fields for the projects of creation; defending at all costs a harmonious sharing between man and his surroundings (even more specifically, nature); extending the right of creation towards all individuals; breaking the fictive barriers imposed by the creation of the nation-states; fomenting broad and solid communication among all creators in the world as base of a human communication among equals.

Thus, if indeed the struggles for national liberation generated the emergence of a certain type of cultures of resistance in different countries,[17] in countries like ours, on borders like ours, the justification of folklore in the terms here outlined would seem to inaugurate the emergence of other new, different, necessary cultures of resistance.

Notes

[1]H. Lewis Morgan, *La sociedad primitiva*. Bogota, Colombia: Ayuso, 1980.

[2]Edward B. Taylor, "La ciencia de la cultura," in *El concepto de cultura: textos fundamentales,* Barcelona, Spain: Anagrama, 1975, pp. 29-46. Here also see the text by Leslie A. White, "El concepto de cultura," pp. 129-55.

[3]I have developed this theme in my previously unpublished work "*Constructing* Regional Cultures" (pp. 79-92 of this book).

[4]Louis-René Nougier, *En los orígenes del trabajo*, Barcelona, Spain: Grijalbo, 1974. Serge Sauneron and Paul Garelli, *El trabajo bajo los primeros estados,* Barcelona, Spain: Grijalbo, 1974. J. A. Giannotti, *Orígenes de la dialéctica del trabajo,* Madrid, Spain: Comunicación, 1973.

[5]"Folklore can be understood only as a reflection of the conditions of cultural life of the people, if indeed some conceptions themselves of

folklore are prolonged even after the conditions have been (or seem) modified or have given place to capricious combinations." In Gramsci, *Antología* (Mexico City: Siglo XXI, 1970, p. 488). On this theme, see in particular L. M. Lombardi Satriani, *Antropología cultural* (Buenos Aires, Argentina: Galerna, 1975).

[6]To understand "accidentality" of the border, with a criticism correlative to the concept of the nation, one can consult Leopoldo Mármora, *El concepto socialista de nación* (Mexico City: Pasado y Presente, 1986), and Rudolf Rocker, *Nacionalismo y cultura* (Madrid, Spain: Las Ediciones de La Piqueta, 1977). Here, our thesis has to do with the fact that borders between nations are the result of political acts and not, so to say, natural divisions.

[7]Tino Villanueva, ed. *Chicanos* (Mexico, City: FCE, 1980). In reality, my argument in this respect is very schematic here. Because of this I am working on a closer analysis of how, until now, the border relation has been conceived between the United States and the population of Mexican descent. There, I believe, I shall give form to my judgments in this respect; at least, the analysis will be a bit longer.

[8]Horkheimer has placed special emphasis on the society-nature correlations in his text "Observaciones sobre la antropología filosófica," contained in *Teoría crítica* (Buenos Aires, Argentina: Amorrortu, 1974, pp. 50-75). From this source I have taken some related ideas. Little by little, other writers are now beginning to make relevant contributions.

[9]I am not ignoring other important books in this respect, such as that of Weigle on kinship or Manuel Peña on music; but studies of this subject remain scarce.

[10]John O. West, *Mexican-American Folklore* (Little Rock, AL: August House, 1988).

[11]It is significant that Anglo Saxon culture is as syncretic as Mexican, which derives from a mixing. Another process is broached that has hardly begun to come to light: *how* the mixing will occur, if it does,

of cultures of apparently such diverse origins. Hence, studies of border folklore should be not overlook this feature.

[12]I insist here on Horkheimer's text and also—to analyze the theme more broadly—on Alfred Schmidt's book *El concepto de naturaleza en Marx* (Mexico City: Siglo XXI, 1976). Beyond the purely ecological foci, one must go towards a more political vision of the question in terms that, for example, Enzensberger suggests.

[13]Apart from reading and consulting specific books on the population of the continent, one should read works such as Mircea Eliade's *El chamanismo* (Mexico City: FCE, 1960), or Mary Douglas's *Pureza y peligro: un análisis de los conceptos de contaminación y tabú* (Madrid, Spain: Siglo XXI, 1973). That is, I refer to the comparative analyses of practices and customs between the most ancient peoples who have existed and those who today exist in isolation.

[14]Henri Lefebvre, *De lo rural a lo urbano* (Barcelona, Spain: Península, 1971). "When the ancient social structures characterized by the existence of a rural nobility gave way to the *polis*, the forms of urban life constituted the model of explanation of the world . . . the new thought is conditioned by the paradigm of a planned and systematic action, normatively regulated, proper for the citizen in a specialized productive activity and a rigorous community order." Ernst Topitsch, "El pensamiento mitológico," in *El concepto de ideología* (Buenos Aires, Argentina: Amorrortu, 1971, pp. 75-83).

[15]Mario Margulis, "La cultura popular," in Adolfo Colombres, ed., *La cultura popular* (Mexico City: Premia, 1982, pp. 41-65).

[16]Here I am thinking basically of unpublished and already published texts of Guillermo Gómez Peña, Harry Polkinhorn, Leobardo Saravia, and Humberto Félix Berumen. Although some are Chicano, others Anglo, and others Mexican, ideas are shared, and similar suggestions are made. See numbers 1, 2, and 3 of *La línea quebrada* edited by Gómez Peña, Polkinhorn, and Hicks; *Esquina Baja* edited by Saravia and Berumen, and the book *La línea: ensayos sobre literatura*

fronteriza, edited by Polkinhorn, *et al.* (Calexico, California/Mexicali, Baja California: Binational Press, 1988).

[17]Amilcar Cabral, "La cultura, fundamento del movimiento de liberación," in Colombres, pp. 137-43.

Cultural Politics in the Present: A Regional Focus

In memory of Guillermo Bonfil Batalla:
longing to argue with him

> Art is useful and necessary for human life, just as bread, meat, fruit, water, and air are . . .
>
> —Diego Rivera, *Art and Politics*

1

I should clarify that perhaps when these notes are read the fantasy of the Free Trade Agreement will have become a reality, just as the unequal relation between Mexico and the United States—in questions having to do with the economy, politics, or culture—is increasingly present. In fact, one of the assumptions of this work is that the relations between Mexico and the United States are increasingly disparate. The eventual signing of the NAFTA would imply only the formalization of these relations. With or without the NAFTA, these relations are definitely those that the current times demand, manifesting themselves as subsidiary to all that which is related to Canada.

In other words, the regional politics of the country should undoubtedly already have been set by the above-mentioned reality, that is, by the fact that between Mexico and the United States contacts, exchanges, and correlations are increasing, especially through this decade and taking as a basis the current hegemonic model of social development (Moreno 1992). How does the above influence the design of a cultural politics in the case of contemporary Mexico?

2

I believe it is important to take into consideration that the relations between Mexico and the United States make the social reality relevant which is concretized in this zone or region known as the northern border, because it would seem to be the paradigm toward which Mexican society is evolving, maintaining the current model of socioeconomic development (Bonfil Batalla 1991).

Also, there is the problem of national culture, knowing what will happen with this to the degree that relations between Mexico and the United States intensify, more so even if sooner or later the NAFTA comes about. Perhaps, we should take the trouble to recall that ours is a pluricultural society, where the notion of national culture is increasingly less operative. Instead, what counts is the existence of cultural singularities in the interior of a society whose stratification begins with the economic but is also manifested in the ethnic, in the religious, and in the geopolitical. Even that patriotic history which all Mexicans held in common is now seen to be disappearing as educated federalization advances in order to bear down upon regional questions with its substantial weight. The national evades unity, seeking diversity.

Nor is the presupposition a central problem of cultural politics. Funds to promote culture will always be lacking.[1] The problem, ultimately, is what to do with the much or the little that exists to give energy to the artistic and cultural life of a country, assuming that these, together with the education, are an unavoidable investment for any contemporary society.

Thus, we begin with the supposition or working hypothesis that the northern border of the country is where the relations with the United States are manifested with the greatest emphasis. Therefore, what happens on this border can serve as a basis for thinking about what future awaits us when culture is discussed.

3

First, let us briefly establish a historical framework to approach the theme of how to design a cultural politics in current Mexico, taking as a basis the growing presence of the relations between Mexico and the U.S. Afterwards, as we shall see, we shall inquire whether there has been a cultural politics in contemporary Mexico and how it has been manifested. Finally some propositions in this respect will be formulated.

Thus, I believe that the remote antecedent of Mexico-U.S. relations—such as these began to acquire their current form (Moyano 1985)—has much to do with the territorial division that the Treaty of Guadalupe Hidalgo formalized in 1846. In this treaty, the development of cultural relations between both countries was not contemplated, perhaps because it was becoming a reality and ultimately it was not considered right to mention such matters in the formal aspects of a document that only acknowledged that a part of the Mexican territory of that time would remain in the power of the U.S. But as Griswold del Castillo (1990) has well showed, in this epoch, this document was rejected precisely because it completely ignored the persistence of Mexican culture in the annexed territories, which those who remained behind and lived there after the annexation considered an affront. Cultural relations between the two countries have taken on a form that is increasingly influential in the daily life of both nations.

With the border relocated to the north of what is now California, border relations between Mexico and the United States could be considered scarce and intermittent (Weber 1988). When the border runs to the Rio Grande and the Colorado River, border relations between the two countries have become increasingly complex and determinative for the social development of both nations. Today, for both countries, these relations are strategic, including their variability and instability. In the framework mentioned above, there are three key questions which I would like to consider at the time of designing a cultural politics for contemporary Mexico: border, migration, and transculturalization.

4

The singularity of the northern border has various elements that I have previously mentioned but which it's worth the trouble briefly to touch on here: desert, urban centers, and exchanges of ways of life and of language.

That is, for current Mexico the relevance of the border in cultural terms has to do not only with the increment of the relations between Mexico and the U.S. but also with the fact that the northern border of this country has recently begun to be identified as a different region within the territorial framework of Mexico.[2] The arid-American region, where the northern border zone of Mexico is located, is geographically different from the central plateau and the zone of the humid tropics of the south and southeast of the country. This geographical differentiation explains why the culture generated in this region is substantially different from that of the other regions of the country. From the period that diverse natural conditions have existed, the transformation of this nature implied differentiated forms of work and finally the manifestation of different forms of social organization (Pugliese 1983). Thus, ascribing relevance to the desert as generator of differentiated cultural dynamics not only results in privileging and differentiating the landscape but also in recognizing that the environment generates different cultural pathways (G6mez Montero 1985).

The other element that bears on the characterization of the northern border of Mexico has to do with the development in it of certain urban centers. When they concentrate economic activity, they become enclaves where cultural manifestations achieve singularity and impact. In this sense, the case of Baja California would seem to be the most exemplary, since its urban centers concentrate 91% of the population, characterizing its daily life by urban hegemony where migration, subordinate industrialization (the *maquila*), and explosive urban growth are the constants that impress their stamp on all the life of the state. Tijuana stands out by its exacerbation of the urban on this border (Alegría 1990).

At the other pole of the border is located Baja California Sur, the least populous state in Mexico. Life in its interior mountain areas follows nineteenth-century patterns. The coastal cities of this state show evidence of the brutal effects of transculturalization. Los Cabos is the paradigmatic example in this respect.

Finally, how is the border modified by what adjoins it? That is, Mexico's northern border shared with California is one thing, but the border we share with Arizona, New Mexico, and Texas is more peaceful and tranquil (with the exception of certain urban centers like Nogales, Ciudad Juárez, and Reynosa).

Border reality also has to do with the construction of a social environment marked by the flows of population that occur between both countries. This movement generates marginal ways of life, some related to resistance and social marginalization: the *cholos*, punks, and surfers (Valenzuela 1988). By contrast, some ways of life are related to the liberality and anonymity which predominate on the border. This attracts tourism, but it also gives rise to a chaotic, fragmented, and unacceptable life characteristic of cities in which privileged zones, bars, night centers, bordellos, and prostitution are permitted and almost officially legalized. Such activities happen literally everywhere as a part of daily life (not counting, of course, the demure, conservative, moralistic, and oftentimes hypocritical segments of society which oppose these practices).

The business done with men, women, and children (some Mexicans, others not) attempting to cross into the United States without documents is also marginal and forbidden. This trafficking has created a police culture in which the principle players are the *"migra"* (U.S. Border Patrol), Mexican police, *"pollos"* (smugglers), and *"polleros"* (the smuggled).

Other typical cultural forms from the border are code language and syncretism. Codes—the graffiti of the *cholos*—are a language of resistance; linguistic syncretism originates in migration, generating a rich market of dialects, and in the structuring of polylingualism whose reason for being is the life in the community of ethnic minorities of multiple origins all along the border zone, although particularly in the part that corresponds to the United States. Specifically, I am here referring to Spanish and English, a mixture of both and, finally, a growing mixture of these two languages with other languages spoken and written by other minorities.

Another element that comprises border cultural reality is migration, which gives life to the entire existence of a culture that does not ever cease restructuring itself. Indeed, the structuration of this reality continuously changes and generates the existence of a floating population. In 1990 in Baja California, according to the XI Population Census, 47% of the residents of the state had been born outside of it. The rate of population growth between 1980 and 1990 was 3.6% annually, that is, one of the highest in the country.

It is certain that the Census facts do not reflect the dimension of migration, nor the problem that this causes in the border states where crossing into the United States is intermittently growing. I am referring to Baja California and Chihuahua. This migration is brought about by various social problems. They have to do with the planning of the urban infrastructure as well as with the provision of services such as education. Not only are questions of quantity involved (how to attend to a floating population, which includes a good deal of children) but also more specifically cultural questions lead to the breakup of customs and traditions linked to the place of origin and the confrontation with and adaptation to forms of culture that are totally new and different (Garduño 1989).

Finally, border reality has to do with transculturalization. This is not a simple transculturalization, however, but a very complex kind. First there is the perverse dynamic having to do with the universalization of the ways of life proper to the society of consumption, whose paradigm is the *American way of life*. This is not only a phenomenon proper to or characteristic of the border but one that more often than not has to do with the spreading of a universalizing culture through information, affecting the cities of the border as well as those of the interior of the country or even small rural populations. Studies so far done in this regard (Bustamante 1982; Castellanos and López y Rivas 1981) indicate that the big cities are the most sensitive to this transculturalization and that, in terms of social stratification, it is those sectors of the population with the greatest economic resources which are the most permeated with the habits of consumption (Douglas and Isherwood 1990).

Less studied is the other kind of transculturalization, having to do with the growing existence of a Mexican-origin population in the United States. If indeed the Spanish-speaking population in California now represents approximately 28% of the population of this state (7.5 million persons), maintaining the historical tendencies approximately until the year 2010 the Spanish-speaking will be a bit more than 50% of the population of this state (Sánchez Soler 1991). Hence we see a cultural process charged with special aspects, in which cultural syncretisim stands out (Gómez Montero 1989). We also note here as a tendency the extension of an amorphous Mexican culture existing fundamentally in the state of California.

5

I have first wanted to mention some elements that mark the specialness of the present time in terms of culture for Mexico, before speaking directly about what the cultural politics of this country have been and are. Thus, the first polemical point has always been to determine if an express State cultural politics exists, or if what happens is such an isolated case that it is not explicitly manifested as the State eagerly hurries to present itself as a *non-intervening factor* in the areas of the freedom of creation. In a certain sense both claims are valid. On the one hand, the State in Mexico in the present century has shown itself resistant to manifest in an express way what it understands as culture and how it promotes culture through a specific politics. On the other hand, it is also certain that the State resists formulating express policies, contributing in effect to preserving freedom of creation (within evident limit). Thus is comprised, like it or not, a cultural politics proper to the State, concretized in practice developed through the operation of the apparatuses that administer different cultural activities in the country.

But the State's cultural politics are not unique. The State permits spaces to be opened in which other institutional actors of the community also intervene in practice to impose cultural standards and behavior on large sectors of the population. This creates a separate cultural politics, whose objectives do not always coincide with those of the State. I am referring to the cultural politics of universities, those generated by the mass media (especially television), and those incipient and stingy cultural politics of the foundations of private capital. The individual, isolated work of artists and groups has been a constant in the recent history of Mexican culture. Here we see the country's most persistent cultural politics. Only recently have we been able to note in State cultural as well as institutional politics the integration into their cultural projects of the new social reality. This reality is characterized, in cultural questions, by the growing presence of the intensification of relations between Mexico and the United States, which would finally be institutionalized with the signing of the NAFTA.

Thus, both explicitly and implicitly, post-Revolutionary Mexican cultural politics have been marked by this ambiguity between a State that apparently does not want to intervene but which in practice has intermittently supported the spread of artistic activities in the country. Indeed, at times the State has been almost the sole support for such activities, aware perhaps that culture is an unavoidable sustenance of politics, as Jesús Reyes Heroles used to say.

Thus, as is said in *Nexos* 173, the Mexican State has been distinguished in this century as finally having given life to mural painting, symphonic music, the mass distribution of good literature, and contemporary dance. If the cost of this politics has brought about controversies over the administrative control of the cultural apparatuses, let us say that this was the price associated with a cultural politics of such a nature.

What is more difficult to explain, however, is the neglect shown by the State toward promoting a true regionalization of cultural activities regarding the pluriculturality of the country. This regionalization has been preoccupied with equitably distributing throughout the nation the resources that the State has destined for the promotion of culture and thereby avoiding the aberrant centralism still ruling in cultural questions.

In this sense, one should recognize that the Borders Cultural Program has been an insufficient mechanism in terms of cultural decentralization and regionalization, but its force is there. In order to value it, one must criticize and above all support it with the goal of making it adequate to the current needs implicit in the country's social development.

What is perhaps not justifiable is the State's passivity when supervising—and to be precise sanctioning—the politics implicit in the use of the mass media. The social costs of these hidden policies produce concrete practices from which no one escapes. Although it is certain that their negative effects have been exacerbated in recent history, nevertheless they have existed for some time now. These policies are identified with the Mexican cinema that apologizes for the Porfirian hacienda that called on people to adopt the life of the poor, that of the prostitutes or of singers. There is little point in revisiting the harm that television is doing to the country (Esteniou 1992). As has been rightly said, television is the true Secretary of Education in Mexico.

Linked to the above, I would like very briefly to mention the existence of other cultural practices that occur indistinctly in the great cities or in specific regions of the country, comprising universes of culture that hegemonize the daily life of these cities or regions. I cite the cultural practices of the middle class of the Federal District, whose emblem is consumption that irrationally imitates the ways of life massified in the United States. Also there is narcoculture, as a manifestation of resistance to the prevailing state of things, and which makes of the villain a social hero in the manner of *Chucho el Roto*.* Finally, I would note the existence of those sectors of the population who see in the indigenous past a point of national identification and struggle, but whose viability today is null and void.

Popular culture is placed in the framework of an unrevealed politics and on the polarized spectrum that runs from the elite to the popular. On its surface popular culture is identified with the processes of manipulation of the mass media. Eventually popular culture is separated off from the State through elite promotion of figures constructed by the media themselves. The appearance of the singer Juan Gabriel in the Palace of Fine Arts is an example of how far this policy has gone.

It is also necessary, however, to point out the force of the deep cultural currents of the Mexican people, sometimes identified with religiosity as a way of thinking and acting. These currents are concretized in ritual and ceremonial practices of a very diverse nature, in the persistence of traditional (herbal) medicine, and in the stubborn survival of 54 indigenous ethnic groups. So we may conclude that the cultural politics of the post-Revolutionary Mexican State have privileged administrative, bureaucratic management of culture, occasionally successfully supporting artistic creation but centralizing the resources and usually overlooking the promotion of the deep cultural currents of the national mainstream.

By contrast, cultural activities promoted by the private sector in Mexico have also existed as constants, particularly from 1950 to the present. These have above all utilized the mass media, generating an induced behavior among ample sectors of the population (Gubern 1987). These activities in practice integrate a cultural politics parallel to the State. Given these considerations, what perspectives give an inkling for present-day Mexico?

6

Here is how Guillermo Bonfil Batalla put it in 1991 (17-18):

> . . . the idea that globalization is the most powerful tendency and the only one that defines the future of our country (as well as that of the rest of the world), seems to be the predominant idea . . . it is a conviction consequent upon the deep anxieties of the colonial mentality: globalization signifies the definite surpassing of the problems that this deep part of our reality suggests, which has stopped us from being truly modern, that is, fully western, without taking on the cultural ballast of the Indian . . . That this way of understanding things exists and pretends to impose itself as the hegemonic vision to define our national project is something that is proven day after day. The current debate over the entrance of Mexico into a common market with the United States and Canada has given place to declarations and assertions that leave no room for doubt over which is the conviction that generates influential parts of the private sector, and also of the government.

As Bonfil himself recognizes, to overcome the fatalism of the above conceptions implies ". . . guaranteeing the intellectual environment (in the broad, unrestricted sense), constructing an authentic vision of ourselves, and conducting the debate over our future through conceptions and identifications closest to reality" (13).

How do we achieve the above in the case of current cultural politics? In this sense, we must understand that culture cannot be restricted only to the territory that privileges ". . . activities, attitudes, tastes, and knowledge of artistic creation, and to a limited field of intellectual activity" (Bonfil Batalla:159), but that we have to open up culture to fields in which it has not entered or has done so insufficiently, above all integrating it into a cultural politics. I think that cultural politics, understood as a specific field of social reality, and particularly of state and governmental reality, has to do with the use of free time, the professionalization of art and cultural workers, the development of a politics that impels the integral formation of individuals, and finally with the decentralization and regionalization of cultural tasks.

Some of the characteristics of how I conceive the fields of the new cultural reality herein mentioned follow. According to Marcuse (1968), the use and enjoyment of free time lead to an awareness of the new routines of productive work in contemporary societies. Physical labor is scant and highly specialized. The individual who works is subject to physical and above all nervous exhaustion. To counteract these forces, in his free time he must completely separate himself from the routines of productive work, in order thus to be reintegrated into the best conditions not only of work but also of daily life in general. Similarly, as the number of workers directly involved in production diminishes, there is an increasingly greater sector of the population whose free (or non-productive) time grows. To avoid conflicts of a social character, this free time must find a creative use in terms of non-productive work (Kogan 1986). The construction of systems of schools for the artistic formation of children, youths, and adults is an example of how to offer valid options to make use of this free time.

A second moment for the new cultural politics is professionalization not only of artistic but also of cultural work in a broader sense. That is, on the one hand artistic work is a social function necessary to contemporary societies intent on channeling the energies generated by free time toward activities that will not negatively react upon the community itself. This makes artistic activities socially necessary functions. Next is the issue of defining who should finance artistic activities in order for them better to accomplish their goals. An equitable distribution of surplus value created by productive work should be legally sought. Artistic and cultural work should be adequately remunerated so that it ceases to be a mere hobby or an occasional or marginal activity.

In this regard, when we speak of the broad sense of cultural practices we want to emphasize the fact that these include not only artistic and a limited intellectual activity but also the spread and promotion of reading as a daily practice. In addition, we include cultural activities on the level of the neighborhood, the group, region, or ethnic group. These activities also include the socially non-injurious use of the mass media.

Education is also a focus. In the following line of cultural politics, we see a need for an integrated formation of the human individual, in such a way that this education opens spaces in which other forms of expression of the human are also manifested. Today such a formation is not adequately attended to. I refer in particular to education in the arts and to physical education. These are seen not as special activities but as annexed to the integrated education of individuals, and indeed they are necessary elements of this education.

Finally, there is the aspect that perhaps most directly concerns those of us who speak from outside the metropolises. I refer to *decentralization* and *regionalization* of culture as processes that drive the three lines mentioned above and respond in a strict sense to the cultural vocations that the different regions of our country have. If indeed these regions are geographically found in the humid tropics, the central plateau, and the arid-American desert, singularities can be identified that create differences and therefore call forth different artistic and cultural activities. To achieve this regionalized development of culture, local and state resources destined to that end must be increased. At the same time, more federal resources should be directed towards the periphery. 80% of the allocation destined by the federal government for culture should *not* go on being invested in the Federal District. It should be more clearly understood that the Fine Arts and CONACULTA are *national* institutions and not metropolitan ones concentrated in the Federal District (SEP 1988; *Zurda* 1989). Clearly, we are dealing not only with resources but also with awareness and behavior. That is, state and municipal governments must be sensitized to their obligations to care for culture more responsibly and enthusiastically.

In terms of cultural politics, one should dismiss the argument over whether or not culture should be supported. All human activity is cultural in its origin. In some such sense, cultural politics would be strengthened if its own practices were to acquire a community character, and not one that is stratifying or discriminatory in terms of social cohesion. Also, I want to pass over that argument over the existence or not of a national culture, stating merely that such a culture cannot exist in a country which in spite of everything continues to be multiethnic and multicultural.

Rather, designing a cultural politics in Mexico calls for preserving our multiculturality in the face of tendencies that preach globalization as a cultural practice to which it is impossible to oppose oneself if one wants to be *modern* (or so they say).

Mexican cultural politics is divided against itself. On the one hand, it emphasizes our varied cultural roots, and on the other hand it wants culture to contribute toward an ever more just, balanced, and less economically polarized society. Thus, cultural politics, in Jesús Reyes Heroles's formulation, is a weapon, the best weapon, of political politics.

Notes

[1]In general terms, cultural proposals inscribed in educational costs amount to less than 1% of this social expense. Nor should one forget that between 1982 and 1987 the amount destined for education nationally went from 5.5% of the GNP to only 3.6%; the per capita in education and per student served in the national educational system for these years decreased from $7,000 to $4,000 and from $23,821 to $14,393, in real 1982 pesos (Prawda 1987). Baja California directed 39.3% of its budget to education in 1982, 37% in 1986, and 39.1% in 1992. For this last year, the state directed 9,000 million pesos to culture, which represented less than 1% of the total allocation for education.

[2]Studies of North American researchers have emphasized this aspect. The relevant bibliography can be found in my work "Border: Space, Time, and Postmodernity" (pp. 163-74 of the present volume).

---

*Mexican Robin Hood.

References

Alegría, Tito. "Ciudad y transformación en la frontera de México con Estados Unidos," in *Frontera norte,* No. 4 (1990), 7-38.

Bonfil Batalla, Guillermo. *Pensar nuestra cultura.* Mexico City: Alianza, 1991.

Bustamante, Jorge. "Uso del idioma español e identidad nacional." Mexico City: CEFNOMEX, 1982 (mimeo).

Castellanos Guerrero, Alicia, and Gilberto López y Rivas. "La influencia norteamericana en la cultura de la frontera norte de México," in Roque González Salazar, *La frontera del norte.* Mexico City: El Colegio de México, 1981.

Douglas, Mary, and Baron Isherwood. *El mundo de los bienes.* Mexico City: CONACULTA/Grijalbo, 1990.

Esteinou, Javier. "¿Comunicación avanzada o retroceso humano?" *Revista CONAFE,* No. 6 (1992), 34-9.

Garduño, Everardo, Efraín García, and Patricia Morán. *Mixtecos en Baja California.* Mexicali, Baja California: UABC, 1989.

Gómez Montero, Sergio. "Frontera: espacio, tiempo y postmodernidad (borradores)." Mexicali, Baja California: UPN, 1990 (mimeo); published here as "Border: Space, Time, and Postmodernity," pp. 163-74.

_____. "Folklore, frontera y resistencia." Mexicali, Baja California: UPN, 1989 (mimeo); published here as "Folklore, Resistance, and the Border," pp. 93-104.

_____. "Para *construir* las culturas regionales." Mexicali, Baja California: UPN, 1986 (mimeo); published here as "*Constructing* Regional Cultures," pp. 79-92.

Griswold del Castillo, Richard. *The Treaty of Guadalupe Hidalgo.* Norman: University of Oklahoma Press, 1990.

Gubbern, Roman. *El simio informatizado.* Madrid, Spain: Fundesco, 1987.

Kogan, Jacobo. *Filosofía de la imaginación.* Buenos Aires, Argentina: Paidós, 1986.

Marcuse, Herbert. *El hombre unidimensional.* Mexico City: Mortiz, 1968.

Moreno, Prudenciano. "La política económica de la modernización educativa," *Pedagogía,* Vol. 8, No. 1 (1992), 6-21.

Moyano, Angela. *México y Estados Unidos: orígenes de una nexos.* Mexico City: 173, 1992, pp. 5-18.

Prawda, Juan. *Logros, inequidades y retos del futuro del sistema educativo mexicano.* Mexico City: Grijalbo, 1989.

Pugliese, Orlando. "'Estado de naturaleza,' relatividad cultural y universalidad científica." Mexico City, 1987 (mimeo).

SEP. *Programa de trabajo del subsector cultura.* Mexico City: SEP, 1988.

Valenzuela, José Manuel. Mexico City.: COLFRON, 1988.

Weber, David. *La frontera norte de México, 1821-1846.* Mexico City: FCE, 1988.

Zurda, Nos. 5-6 (1989).

Literature and History: Models to Provide

1

Given a recent rebirth of history in literature (especially in fiction, in Mexico and other countries), we can see how reflections on the complex relations that occur between both analytical practices gain relevance. Also, we can see how, at the level of the product, both history and fiction are increasingly confused. In fact, at least two problems are involved. One is the specificity of both fields of study (not excluding their evident relations). Following on conceiving intellectual practices as a network of circuits of communication (which impacts similarly the first problem), a second problem is the specificity of language required to concretize practices of both historical and literary writing. Hence, the object of these notes is to suggest a brief and summary investigation into one of the aspects of the first nucleus of problems, the evident relations between history and literature and how an analytical approach to them should be realized.

2

The real problem of the evidence is that even though it is always there oftentimes we don't see it. We pass it over, or we overlook the importance of its existence. Hence, if in fact one must accept the clear relations between history and literature, one navigates against the wind in trying to establish what type these relations are and how they are manifested. I do not want to try to exhaust the theme. Rather, I shall point out two specific moments of these relations and how the knowledge of them can be a basis for timely reflections and analyses of the material under consideration.

In a first moment we begin with the principle that all literary writing is real and therefore historical. This leads, of necessity, to a determination of how literature is historical insofar as it is real, without falling into the trap of crude historicism. Without subdivisions, literature is thus joined to its given social time. A knowledge of the literary is developed, connecting it univocally with the simple evolution of social time (an example of this is socialist realism). If we really want to study the relations between history and literature, one should here introduce a hypothesis that establishes differences, first between subject (who writes, who transmits orally) and object (written or oral product), in order to recognize the existence of different mechanisms for measuring the interrelated transformation of subject and object. This, in turn, leads to the conception of the literary as social fact with diachronic changes that move very slowly within history (the transformation of society through work). Diachronically, the product has been transformed more rapidly because it increasingly forms part of the circuit of commodities. Synchronically, the changes have also been slighter regarding the subject, since the object (to the degree that its discourse spans the distance between the individual's interiority and the community) suffers noticeable transformations.

While historicism, then, establishes a mechanical relation between literature and history (the aberrations of Zdanov; some of Plejanov's ideas; Lafargue; the Lukacs of Stalinism), a more useful vision in terms of verification is that which offers specificity to the literary exercise, simultaneously acknowledging the specificity of the subject and the product, in order later to recognize that the literary object is not only one, but that it unfolds in at least three great practices: poetry, narrative, and essay. The link of these practices with history is also differentiated. I will consider only a few differences in the connection: while poetry is basically denomination, it in fact would seem to be unchanging in the face of time and its insertion in history (society conceived as movement). I believe this has to do with the step from the oral to the written more than with possible changes suffered by poetry's nominative function. Fiction, in contrast, insofar as it is fabulation, descriptive of adventures, has a more precise historical charge, above all since the time when history or daily life was anthropomorphized, and therefore its subject matter had to do with immediacy or with the recuperation of daily life of other times. The historical novel is situated at exactly this point. The essay, on suggesting all the processes of abstraction in this respect, has to do equally with literary practice, with history conceived here as epistemological practice and with history which seeks to assimilate and interpret reality (not simple reality but complex reality). To validate itself, the essay can say that literature is *more* history but *not history as a whole* (again, a historicist reduction of literature). Literature, however, has its own specificity. What follows is a reflection on the specificity of the literary essay and its connection with history.

3

In "The Theory of the 'Formal Method'," Eikhenbaum writes that we have, in the formalist, ". . . the desire to create an autonomous literary science starting with the intrinsic qualities of literary materials. Our only object is the theoretical and historical awareness of the facts that depend on literary art as such." For his part, glossematics (since Hjelmslev) is still preoccupied with finding the specific markers of the "literary" text. In his elaborately structuralist "The Autonomy of the Aesthetic Process," Badiou shows that art in its disquisitions is not ideology or science but a specific field—real and concrete—of human creation. Yes, but how?

In fact, in order to find its *raison d'être*, art (literature here) ambitiously seeks to establish its specificity and knows that it alone will be able to achieve it by complying with a prerequisite: being inscribed in history. The problem is *how* to be inscribed in history without forcing its essence or, therefore, its existence. Art's existence is forced when it is marginalized from history, located on the edge of it (on top of it or to one side of it). Its essence emerges when art confronts and competes with history. How can we avoid these dilemmas? In the Lukacsian manner of transcending the opposition between essence and appearance?

My proposal has already been mentioned: to define literature dialectically as a specific circuit of communication, which is subdivided into at least three specific concrete practices. The third of these, the literary essay, has abstraction (i.e., thinking in order to know) as a basis for its functioning. The essay wants to establish the "in and of itself" of the literary fact (the literary fact, that is, of a specific segment of reality, not of all reality, nor in competition with other processes of abstraction that are approached in the study of other specific segments of reality).

Now then, if the essay complies with this specific function, how has it been able to achieve this function? How does the essay reduce reality, assimilating it by a process of abstraction? We turn to epistemology for a response, even though epistemology's responses have not always been altogether satisfactory. Hence, as a process of abstraction the literary essay is submitted and related to epistemology, although without losing its specificity. To repeat, we are granting to literature a compartmentalization and a historical determination. A first function of the literary essay is to demonstrate the validity of the above. A second function is to explore the *how* of literature, its methodology.

Of course the above sketch does not "discover America." I offer it merely as a referential framework for the study of literature, a framework constructed of constantly changing different experiences. In principle, all reduction of reality to abstraction gives rise to a model which reproduces reality only to a limited extent. To establish the validity of the model, some factors to consider are which elements of reality were abstracted and what importance is given to each of them. One should not forget, moreover, that we are talking of a fragmented reality (in this case, literature). Hence, the model proposed reproduces, first, a circuit of communication, and second, the historical context in which this circuit is inserted. Simplified to the maximum, this circuit includes sender, language, code, message-object, and receiver, which create an interacting conjunction of networks acquiring more or less importance according to the context in which the circuit is inserted. Thus, the task of the essay is to determine which dimension should receive greatest importance: the circuit, some of its elements, or the historical context. How do we equilibrate the circuit and context within the model?

References

Althusser, Louis, et al., eds. *Literatura y sociedad.* Buenos Aires, Argentina: Tiempo Contemporáneo, 1974.

Chklovski, Victor, ed. *Formalismo y vanguardia.* Madrid, Spain: Comunicación, 1970.

Eagleton, Terry. *Una introducción a la teoría literaria.* Mexico City: FCE, 1988.

Gallas, Helga. *Teoría marxista de la literataura.* Buenos Aires, Argentina: Siglo XXI, 1973.

Girolamo, Giacomo di. *Teoría crítica de la literatura.* Barcelona, Spain: Crítica, 1982.

An Unseizable Object: The Study of Literature

for Roberto Castillo and *Capo* Di Bella

"The negation that opposes the one and the multiple, as Parmenides opposed Being and Non-Being, is also negation in the sense of a defense before the ingrained and deep anguish in the face of decrepitude and death, isolation and separation, opposition and contradiction, surprise and innovation."

—Habermas, *El pensamiento posmetafísico*

1

The following notes touch on different experiences having to do with my activities as university professor of literature and Spanish language (or, more precisely, Castilian), coordinator of creative writing workshops, and author of a series of lectures. Some of these ideas have already been published. Others form part of an investigation in process.

Consequently, I have taken certain liberties in editing my own work, which at times behaves somewhat disrespectfully towards academic orthodoxy. Rather, I move in two directions. One presents the opinions of the subject who wrote this text and who, from the point of view of his individuality, develops theses and suggests hypotheses. Second, the object of this exercise is to continue a polemic which has existed for some time and which in contemporary times has been renovated and, according to Habermas (199) among others, will soon occupy a very significant place in the terrain of human thought and action: what language do we speak? Its logocentric pretensions reduced, is language always a metaphor? Where does it begin and end as a factor of humanization? Clearly, if literature is language, these questions also are incumbent on literature.

Here, as in other cases, one must begin with certain obvious matters in order to make possible a way through material which is eminently complex and vast. Therefore, there are two sources that I would like to identify as the basis for this text. One is the question to study. The other is the question of literature.

2

Hence, I shall first briefly cross the terrain of the study, treating of the question what it is to study, and above all what an object of study is. As I want to avoid useless erudition, I'll only say that by study I mean the knowledge of something, a process, or a phenomenon (or a subject that *is not* the subject who studies) which bears significantly on the daily life of a subject. This knowledge understands the scholarly process, if indeed it has its reason for historical being,as totally aleatory in the purest epistemological sense.

Thus, in terms of systems theory, to know implies the flowing of information which emerges from a source (which can be an object or a subject) and which, restricted to the human, necessarily reclaims the existence of a subject that assimilates given information, usually giving it new meaning. The educational process has predicated the necessary existence of a subject sender of information as unavoidable requisite for the concretization of knowledge. This has detracted from the study of the literary as creative process with its own, different, other reality, which in fact does not require the existence of this subject sender of information.

Let us avoid a detailed description of the process of knowing whose polemical potential would seem to be interminable. We admit only that knowing is inscribed in a system—and the *whole* is in itself a system—in which sender, language, code, receiver, and context are elements that are analyzed at length to understand the system, the interrelations that occur among its elements, and the interrelations established among the subsystems that integrate the total system.

3

Since when has literature been an object of study? Here I take up again an old discussion which turns among other things on the separation of literature from other social practices (religion and magic), on what to study, language in general or specific language. Is literature poetry, or is it linguistic history and change? Will the formalists and their followers one day be able to find *literariness*, the supposed essence of the literary?

As is known, in *Ion* and above all in the *Republic*, Plato speaks very poorly of poets and destines them to ostracism so that the idea, one day, can dominate daily life. The ordering that Aristotle makes in the *Poetics*—where *catharsis* is a bridge between rational logic and other logics, and where the essence of the literary is rooted—still prevails in good measure, has impact on and conditions scholarly practices. Only much later, with the *Port Royal Grammar* and above all the linguistics of the late nineteenth century (Malmberg 1975), will these practices seek in the study of language and its uses the reason for being of the literary (the study of the subject is decentered as producer, and emphasis will fall again on the product and particularly on its component parts).

Clearly, the object of study has been transformed. Everyone has understood it in his own way, not to say at his own convenience. Still, we find a series of constants: the preeminence of the use of oral and written language as basis of human communication, and from there their systematic study in terms of rhetoric, literature, or linguistics. Hence, literature and aesthetics run parallel. Their values are essentially the same: those that radically separate physical and intellectual work, and specialized human deeds. We see the passage from subject to object (the decentering of which I spoke above), thereby "decontaminating" the object of study of subjectivity. Especially in recent times, periodization as a basis of change accounts for the weight which language has acquired as pivotal in the study of the literary. The above points are constants that are intermittently manifested. Among them they have captured the attention of literary scholars.

In this connection, Plato's comments in the *Laws* (Hall 1982:18) are relevant:

> . . . no one will be able to sing a song that has not been approved by the guardians of the law, although its melody is sweeter than the songs of Tamira and Orpheus; only those poems considered sacred will be sung and those dedicated to the works of good men, in which praise and blame have been allotted, and who, according to judgment, have accomplished their purpose adequately.

That is, in the question "What is literature?" we find enclosed another, more fundamental question: "What has it been?" Thus we are led immediately to admit diversity, polyvalence, and ambiguity in this practice called literature, according to the historical time in which it occurs (Eagleton 1988).

4

Further reflection establishes that theorization of the literary has placed emphasis on the definition of the object of study: on historiographical periodization; on the function of the practice (what is literature good for?); on the essential contents of this practice. Today we are confronted with the unveiling of the logic which originates this practice (Derrida; Eagleton 1988; Ryan 1982; Norris 1990).

I do not want to argue about literature's fallibility but only to reaffirm my belief that the literary object is broad and complex enough to explain the multiplication of approaches to its study and experiencing. One should not forget that not all knowledge comes from study. However—central to this study—for some time there has existed a fundamental confusion which, especially among the learned, has brought the study of literature to an acute crisis it has not yet been able to escape: deconstruction and hermeneutics are increasingly bogged down in metaphysical questions (Ricoeur 1981). This confusion has to do with the unification, in one essence alone, of literary *process* and literary *product* (I don't want to go into the question of the substantial differences among natural language or languages and specialized languages, discourses, if you like; nor into the issue of the tenuous and shifting borders between literature, magic, religion, and neurosis). These, I believe, have contributed to the above-mentioned crisis.

What about literary *process* and *product*? Process has to do with objectified subjectivity, the potentiality of the human being to transcend himself in order to give an objectified part of himself. Only when this objectified part becomes the property (although not in a sense of physical belonging) of *another* (that is, another subject, not that of the originally produced object) does there exist the product. Therefore, the act of creation is socially concretized. It is through the existence of *two* subjects—one conscious of the other—that we can speak of social existence of creation.

Now then, of what *process* and what *product* do we speak in the case of literature? First, we speak of the use of oral language and written language. Second, we speak of the re-signification of common language. Finally, we speak of the imagination (in human subjects). Hence, then, the study of the literary, whether as process or product, implies at least the study of two perfectly differentiated technologies: oral language and written language. Also involved are semantics, and especially communication theory (more generically, systems theory). This leads to the study of subjects as social individuals and also as psychological individuals. Finally, the above also implies a knowledge of phenomenology in order to discern how the imagination is concretized (Lapoujade 1988). If indeed all the above is immersed in and has to do with the literary process and product, it can be studied as *product,* not as *process*. That is, literature as *process* can not be the object of study (or of a process of teaching-learning, if you like). Why? Now I shall turn to the other main part of my thesis.

5

If we admit the existence in literature of two moments—process and product—and place emphasis on the first, we can easily see that it is characterized essentially by its composition. It is the result of an absolute subjectivity. This subjectivity usually leads to a conscious or unconscious break of the form of utilizing language (whether natural or specialized). Finally its quality as a product of the imagination—complex psychic function—leads it continually to individuation. Can this process be the object of teaching and finally of learning if teaching and learning imply a basic regularity and norms?

Before answering the above question, I want to continue examining the literary product. Now almost always a book, at other times the product took the form of *jongleur*'s song. Even further back it was the rhapsodic ode or hymn. Hence, the product has come to be conceived, in and of itself, as invariable. It is, therefore, a source of information that is modified only through its emission or reception, which are complexes made up of the group of elements that intervene in the composition of the object (Rall 1987).

Although I share with Jauss (Rall 1987:59-72) the necessity of constructing new paradigms for the study of the literary, parallel to it, I believe, as I have been arguing, that it is equally significant to begin differentiating literary process from product, in order to be able to see the impossibility of process becoming an object of study. That is, this differentiation forms part of a circuit of communication in which the transmitter (the teacher) can offer to the receiver (the pupil) information (the *process* of literary creation) that this latter can assimilate, systematize, and reproduce.

6

Up to this point I hope I have shared the idea of the necessity of differentiating literary process and product, not only in literature but by implication in all acts of artistic creation. Thus, if we look from the past forwards, we recall that study is the transmission of information, which *the receiver should decode in order to assimilate it and then to apply it in his practice without modifying it.* This is true even in the case of new schemes of teaching, where memorization seeks to be replaced by the reconstruction of the logic or procedure that gave rise to the transmitted information (Zemelman 1987). Still, we find a territory that does not fit in this scheme or model of circuit of communication. This territory is that of creation (Bruner 1988). In particular, it is that of artistic creation in its acceptation as *process,* not as *product* (Davis and Scott 1989). Here I reduce my argument to the case of literary artistic creation, understood as an act of subjectivity which implies a singular use of oral or written language with an imaginative goal (Kogan 1986; Lapoujade 1988). Can this process be the object of study?

We see its basic elements: subjectivity, special use of language, and imagination. In terms of information, how are these transmitted? What's the point of doing so, if they cannot be universalized or integrated into a model (Thom 1987), which today is the paradigm of the processes of teaching-learning? In fact, from the moment that it is the result of the deepest and most firmly rooted subjectivity, of a use where language seeks always to be distinct; and where the image, result of subjectivity, is always other, literary creation as process will be distinguished by being an unrepeatable, unique act, a totally singular and indivisible result of the One (I myself) in its deepest aspect. Hence, this process *can not be taught,* but knowledge of it is acquired through experience and the practical result of individual exercise.

Through some such line of reasoning, one can safely claim that the study of literature *should not center on the process of creation as object of its preoccupations but should be centered on the literary product*. This position can help the practices of literary study to emerge from the crisis in which it finds itself today.

References

Bruner, Jerome. *Realidad mental y mundos posibles*. Madrid, Spain: Gedisa, 1988.

Davis, Gary, and Gary Scott. *Estrategias para la creatividad*. Buenos Aires, Argentina: Paidós, 1989.

Eagleton, Terry. *Una introducción a la teoría literaria*. Mexico City: FCE, 1988.

Habermas, Jürgen. *El pensamiento posmetafísico*. Mexico City: Taurus, 1990.

Hall, Vernon, Jr. *Breve historia de la crítica literaria*. Mexico City: FCE, 1982.

Kogan, Jacobo. *Filosofía de la imaginación*. Buenoes Aires, Argentina: Paidós, 1986.

Lapoujade, María Noel. *Filosofía de la imaginación*. Mexico City: Siglo XXI, 1975.

Norris, Christopher. *What's Wrong with Postmodernism?* Baltimore: The Johns Hopkins University Press, 1990.

Rall, Dietrich, ed. *En busca del texto: teoría de la recepción literaria*. Mexico City: UNAM, 1987.

Ricoeur, Paul. *El discurso de la acción*. Madrid, Spain: Cátedra, 1981.

Ryan, Michael. *Marxism and Deconstruction*. Baltimore: The Johns Hopkins University Press, 1984.

Thom, René. *Estabilidad estructural y morfogénesis: ensayos de una teoría general de los modelos*. Madrid, Spain: Gedisa, 1987.

Zemelman, Hugo. *Historia y política en el conocimiento*. Mexico City: UNAM, 1983.

The Literary Essay in the 29th State (Baja California)

> The metaphor of the code, even when it has been a mere metaphor, at least has always responded to a unifying obsession: the dialectic between law and creativity . . .
>
> —Eco, *Semiotics and Philosophy of Language*

I

The purpose of this study is not to offer a tedious compilation of what the artistic and literary essay has been in Baja California. Others have already done this (Trujillo 1990a). Perhaps the most that can be hoped for is to deepen the investigation of sources.

In fact, therefore, what I attempt here is to identify the motivations, how they have been made dynamic. I am interested in recent tendencies in the literary essay in Baja California. This genre has really only lately begun to appear in the state.

Thus, perhaps the most plausible starting point for an exploration of the literary essay in Baja California is Adorno (1962). With his customary lucidity, he points out that the essay, as a literary genre, does not begin to manifest itself and to mature, except at that moment in which other genres—poetry and fiction—have already advanced and consolidated themselves. The correspondence and interrelation among genres, therefore, is one of the first motivations of a writerly exercise whose specificity and complexity noticeably limit their practice.

That is, to speak of the Baja California literary essay implies turning to the final years of the 1970s and the beginning of the 1980s, when the period of academic-cultural consolidation of state institutions had made the first babblings possible. At this time we saw the appearance of a number of authors born here who were beginning to publish their texts in those places where it was permitted: magazines (*Ultimo vuelo*), cultural sections of newspapers (*Identidad*), and authors' publications (*Fuera del cardumen*). Trujillo himself, in the work cited above, analyzes in great detail the whys and wherefores of this phenomenon.

During this period, for example, the first notes and reviews of Baja Californian literary production begin to appear in nationally distributed newspapers. We have two pamphlets from this time (Bayardo: 1979 and León Zavala: 1982), where the materials gathered already clearly lay out themes leading to reflection and literary analysis. Some of these are the historical origins and development of the literary, the problem of the mixture and syncretization of tongues, and the unequal if symbiotic relation of cultures occurring on the northern border of the country. In fact, I think that reflection—expressed in these essays—was motivated by a phenomenon that was particularly close to the Baja Californians of that time, but not absolutely their own: *chicanismo*, which in the middle of the 1960s and almost all the 1970s strongly manifested its presence in the zone of the North American states neighboring Mexico. This movement captured much attention at the time. Some of the most recognized texts from that period are those of Montoya, Alurista, Villanueva, as well as the work of Polkinhorn and Velasco on Chicano *caló*.

The other strong motivation that dynamized the essay (not to mention the nascent poetry and fiction of that period) was social resistance to a degrading presence of the North American population in the border cities. It's not a question of sovereignty herein discussed, but of the black year when the Marines come to give free rein to the body. Thus, ethical questions are treated. A third, more relevant theme (Zavala 1982:24-32) is the impressionistic analysis of border counter-culture, whose riches were evident, even if the theme was not always treated with the rigor it seemed to demand.

As one can see, the germs of the literary essay in contemporary Baja California were already contained in the works of Zavala and Bayardo. In fact, they can be considered the pioneers of the medium. But the writing of essays is not a simple matter: to write them, apart from an encyclopedic knowledge of the themes under study, a special creative sensibility is required. One of the recurrent vices in this respect was precisely the submitting of the writer to dominant influences and tendencies that rippled through the literary essayists in the country from the center to the periphery. (This was not the only ruling vice at the time. The pejorative way in which reference was made to the essayistic in our country, indicated, although not always rightly so, its weaknesses.)

Thus, centralism made itself felt in this genre, although not with the virulence of other cases (I cite, for example, the fact that even today we see work offered as reference points for Baja Californian literary essays. These are texts datelined in Mexico City or produced by writers from there who speak of the northern border at times with an absolute lack of knowledge of the area). In spite of these limitations and detours, the literary essay in Baja California has broadened and diversified itself and is increasingly established as a solidly structured reflexive exercise.

II

Thus, poetry, fiction, and the essay developed by parallel routes. The first two, however, initiated the new upsurge. In the 1980s the three genres combined to form the literary efflorescence of Baja California, expressed—above all at the end of this period—in a surprising degree of editorial production. One should especially take into consideration that in the years before, faced with the exodus of the youth of the state, there was really very little literary activity here and few books that documented it.

For the essay as for other literary genres, it is possible to identify three areas of publication: newspapers (culture sections), periodical publications (literary-cultural magazines), and books. In order to know works and authors in detail, and to identify tendencies and motivations, one need only consult these documents.

The essay had its foundation in a twofold sense. First was the possibility of publishing. Second was the existence of work and the interchange of experiences, especially among writers of the region. These currents offered ample room for reflecting on literature. However, since then a noticeable limit has made itself evident: in the essay writing does not function only as a reflexive act, but above all as result of a process of enlightenment (academic or not), the essay, with few exceptions, was feeble in its structure, methodology, and contents. Among its faults were a schematic quality, scholastic orthodoxy, impressionism, neopositivist formalism, and superficiality. This assumes established formulas for the genre. The essay needs some minimal elements to justify itself as such (Lucacs 1975; Adorno 1982).

As much in Baja California as in Mexico City, journalism offers perhaps fewer examples of the essay in the strict sense and more of the review, which permits following the course of recently published work, appreciating its basic contents and its most relevant stylistic elements. Here we find no deeper or more formal ambitions, although the review brings together the initial information leading to tasks of a greater reach, of reflection on being in itself of literature. In this respect, contributions have been made by Di Bella, Trujillo, Félix Berumen, and myself (to a lesser degree Hernández and Gutiérrez).

The 1980s in Baja California are the years of the magazines. In good measure, they are the best gauge of the level achieved by literary production in the area. It's not odd, therefore, that here in good measure we find the most significant examples of the genre. *Esquina*

B aja, Hojas, El oficio, La ranura del ojo, La revista de humanidades, Entorno-Arquetipo, Tintas, La línea quebrada, Cultura norte, Melquiades, Trazadura, and *Comunicarte* offer spaces for reflection on literature. In these magazines, the essays is published and cast into high relief, gaining special importance. In addition to the above-mentioned writers, others who should be cited are Saravia, Gómez-Peña, Polkinhorn, Hicks, Vargas, Valenzuela, Contreras, and Espinoza. The genre acquires a status equivalent to fiction and poetry.

Different from the periodical review, the literary essay published in the magazines is distinguished by the attention it gives to the regional as nodal point for reflection. Borderization, symbiosis, alterity, decentralization, the avant-garde, postmodernity, and "mex-u.s.-icization" are concepts (and not only neologisms) that animate the writings of these authors, who attempt to explain the singularity of the literary production of the border. They have tried to show how this production, on differentiating itself, wants to achieve its own *status* of validation.

However, as Escalante (1992), referring to the Baja California essay, says, novelty of concepts is not always sufficient to validate the essay as such. It is sometimes theoretically weak. It often remains on the surface of the thematic treatment, or is formally deficient. Also, we see that the literary essay that appeared in the magazines specialized in fault-finding. This can be attributed to isolation, the attempt to respond to current questions, or haste in composition. Finally, and perhaps most importantly, the essay does not show evidence of knowledge of a previously constructed theoretical *corpus*. Hence, its effects in terms of process of communication (Habermas: 1985) are not always fully achieved. In spite of these shortcomings, its importance on the regional level has been highly significant.

Occupying an intermediate area between the magazine and the book is the essay, prologue, or introduction as found published in anthologies and proceedings. Bridge, witness, or hypothesis, such works have sometimes first appeared in magazines, then later in books, which add further validation to the form. This is especially true if the book retains unity and coherence and is not merely a collection of different writings.

Finally there are the books, really very few, and they not always or entirely have to do with the literary essay. For example, there are books that have only tangentially to do with the literary (Valenzuela 1988; Trujillo 1988). Others bring together more journalistic pieces (Trujillo 1990b).

A last category are those books the core of which is reflection on the literary. One has been commented on by me before (Gómez 1987). Another, more recently issued collection (Bayardo 1990) gathers works previously published (corrected and augmented) and others unpublished. In these books we can more precisely identify the meaning of the reflection on the literary. In the first case we see this operating in general terms. In the second, reflection emerges from the writer's specific interest in Baja Californian literature. One should mention two books now in the process of being completed—one by Trujillo and the other by Gómez—the focus of which is almost entirely on the literature of the 29th state.

III

It can be determined from the above discussion that the object of this study is not an analysis of work, nor is it a bio-bibliographical description of authors. Its objective, rather, is more diffuse: what has the literary essay in Baja California already achieved? This broaches a third and final dimension: perspectives in terms of tendencies.

Here I owe much to Derrida (1984), amplified by Habermas (1989) from the viewpoint of anthropocentric thought, whose pivot is not the grammar of language or the logic of its use. Of relevance, rather, is what Derrida explicitly calls the science of writing, which in Habermas is transformed into a theory of communication, in Eco (1990) into a semiotics of language, and which I call total functioning of the circuits of communication.

A study of totality, of the holistic in the universal abstract-concrete can be conducted based on the facts of the literary essay marked by a regionalism whose territorial demarcation is Baja California. How do we come down to earth from these heights? Simple and complex at the same time, the order of discourse here takes three routes.

The first of these routes is related to the literary work: the essay will be such to the degree that fiction, poetry, and the essay exist on which to reflect (Adorno 1962). *A priori* speculation on the quality of the work does not matter. What the essay requires in the first instance to express itself is only that the work exists. Whatever follows will be extra.

Through the second route the situation is made more complex. In fact, the education of the essayist as such does not respond to formulas and cannot be constrained to the purely academic. If indeed educational preparation is dominant, it is not always a guarantee that only in this way are literary essayists formed. The most palpable example in this respect is our own country, if we take into account indicators such as the following. How many graduates of Mexican schools of literature are essayists? Of the known essayists in Mexico, how many learned their office in the academy? How then are essayists educated? Here I am thinking of a process of reading that must be simultaneously methodical and almost absolute, a kind of reading that approaches all the fields of knowledge (for literature, the paradigmatic example is Kien, Canetti's character in *Auto da fé*). In order to become creative at the time of being expressed in essay form, the essayist will have to have a very precise and concrete knowledge of the historical context in which the work in question has been produced as well as of the context in which it itself, the essay, is written in its twin aspects of produced object and producing subject.

Finally, the third route concerns the produced object—the essay in itself—whose essential characteristic, I feel, is creativity, achieved through a thorough knowledge of the object being reflected upon; who and in what way others have already reflected on this object. Such knowledge makes possible articulation of the problem and reconstruction of the object (Zemelman 1987), and the process of reconstructing the object of study lays the foundation for proposing new problems. Eco's comment below illustrates these points:

> It is appropriate to think of the encyclopedia as a labyrinth which, even if it doesn't admit a global description, neither does it exclude local descriptions, since its character as labyrinth has nothing to obstruct our study of it and our *construction* of its distinct pathways. (my emphases) (1990: 340).

References

Adorno, Theodor W. "El ensayo como forma," in *Notas de literatura,* Madrid, Spain: Ariel, 1962.

Bayardo, Patricio. *Dos ensayos.* Tijuana, Baja California: ITT 1979.

_____. *El signo y la alambrada.* Tijuana, Baja California: Entrelíneas, 1980.

Derrida, Jacques. *De la gramatología.* Mexico City: Siglo XXI, 1984.

Eco, Umberto. *Semiótica y filosofía del lenguaje.* City, Spain: Lumen, 1990.

Escalante, Evodio. "Ventana sucia: ensayos sobre literatura fronteriza," in *Trazadura,* 1 (1990), 86-7.

Gómez Montero, Sergio. *Los caminos venturosos.* Mexicali, Baja California: UABC, 1987.

Habermas, Jürgen. *Teoría de la acción comunicativa.* Vols. I and II. Madrid, Spain: Taurus, 1986.

_____. *El discurso filosófico de la modernidad.* Madrid, Spain: Taurus, 1988.

León Zavala, Ramiro. *Ensayos y relatos*. Tijuana, Baja California: ITT, 1982.

Lukacs, Georg. "Sobre la esencia y forma del ensayo," in *El alma y las formas*.Barcelona, Spain: Grijalbo, 1975.

Trujillo Muñoz, Gabriel. *Tres ensayos sobre el ensayo bajacaliforniano*. Mexicali, Baja California: UABC, 1988.

_____. "La literatura en Baja California: tendencias, propuestas y protagonistas," in *Literatura mexicana,* Vol. 1, No. 2 (1990a), 112-23.

_____. *Alabanzas y vituperios*. Mexicali, Baja California: Author's publication, 1990b.

Valenzuela, José Manuel. *¡A la brava ése!* Mexico City: COLFRON, 1988.

Zemelman, Hugo. *Uso crítico de la teoría*. Mexico City: El Colegio de México, 1987.

Literature and Regionalization in Sonora

for my teacher Francisco Luna

> When someone says something in the form of a generalization extracted from reality, it approximates a dream and, even more, poetry.
>
> —Hofmannsthal, *El libro de los amigos*

1

Analyses of Mexican literature are gradually multiplying, opening up new fields of reflection. Previously latent, these works have been gathering force. In such a historical framework[1] I would position studies that seek to establish the parameters of regionalization in a context that demands a definition of the centralist tendencies that have oppressed the country.

But if indeed the necessity and the demand exist, we have just begun to make advances in this area. On the one hand, priority has been given to the specifically historical and economic to the detriment of other fields of knowledge. On the other hand, in a very slow way people are being trained who are needed in order to do this work.

Literary analysis has placed the emphasis more on questions of a particular character (the analysis of works and authors) than on the context. Therefore, works have submitted to predominating centralist tendencies. In its zeal to give priority to works and authors (over historical context), the country lacks a solid and trustworthy history of its national literature. The referential framework has been neglected which is not a simple enclave of general history but the structure that permits the most telling differentiation of the ontic aspect of the literary.[2] This applies most validly on the national level, but it is also justified in local spheres, such as the states.

I would like here to attempt a first approach towards constructing a spatial frame of reference in which to situate the literary production of the state of Sonora, thereby linking literature with the geophysical sphere in which it appears. What I shall offer is a sketch, a hypothesis I hope will be debated and discussed.

2

The attempt to establish a regionalization of nature being suggested here is not gratuitous, of course. It responds essentially to four more or less defined motives. One is to found the "demetropolitanization" of literary studies on an increasingly solid basis, starting from the supposition that such studies acquire greater strength[3] on passing through the provincial filter. To contribute to the definition of the historical-social framework of the country's different states is my second motive, given that until now literature has not received the attention due it in existing macro-studies.[4] As a result, such work remains relatively incomplete.

In the third place there is that question already mentioned having to do with the necessity of filling a significant vacuum, giving body to a general history of Mexican literature fed precisely by the respective regional histories, each characterized by the rigor of its theoretical and methodological foundations. Finally, a fourth motive places emphasis on the historical spatial core. Neglected in theoretical-analytical terms, this seeks the disappearance of a historicism that has done much harm especially to literary studies.

The above assumptions inform my argument throughout. The root cause for chronicling literature has to do with taxonomies of Aristotelian paternity[5] which Lévi-Strauss lucidly analyzes when he says:

> The significant images of myth, the materials of the *bricoleur,* are elements definable through a double criterion: *they have served* as words of a discourse that mythic reflection "dismantles" in the manner of the *bricoleur* who arranges the mesh of an old dismantled alarm clock; and *they can still* serve for the same use, or for a different use, even though a little different from their original function . . . This logic operates somewhat in the manner of the kaleidoscope: an instrument that also contains scraps and pieces, by means of which cultural orders are realized (emphases in original).[6]

To carry these principles of order—established as much by Aristotle as by Lévi-Strauss—over into the practical, and to apply them to criticism on the regional level, implies several assumptions. One is the relationship between the general and the specific, where the former corresponds to the national and the latter to the marginal or provincial. How do we adjust the former, through a dialectical accumulation of the latter, without this latter losing its own specificity? Is the non-existence of a rigorous national literary history conditional upon the non-existence of rigorous regional literary histories? How is such a national literary history constructed, through a centrist exercise—the dominant tendency until now—or through supporting the construction of this history in the respective provinces? The unavoidable interrelation of the national and the provincial is evident, through the supposition that the former cannot be constructed without the latter, particularly now that the nation is demanding to revert to the centralizing processes that have overwhelmed it since the last century and that seem to have arrived at their greatest invalidity and dysfunctionality in current times.

A second coordinate axis is the social, the characteristics of which have to do with the way in which individuals are interrelated among themselves, in so far as they are members of a collectivity or group. The group of relations generated produces a necessary frame of reference for the study of social facts, as is the case with literature. In this view, differences are identifiable, for example, between the individuals who comprise a nation, at the edges of which common principles of social order exist for these individuals: exploitation, submission, subordination, in summary, speaking of a dominant historical axis, the relations between capital and labor.

The third dimension is history, as articulated through two basic principles: 1) space and time, and 2) the evolution which the work factor has shown.[7] In fact, in this study I will reflect on the significance and transcendence of space in historic-literary terms. But one should not forget that the chronological also comprises, for example, as in periodization, a function of significant importance,[8] where questions arise such as how to differentiate or join historical time and literary time, if both are ruled by different orders. These are questions that indeed address the importance of the theme and in themselves demand the realization of specific works. Now I would like to turn towards the concrete material of this study: physical space as a constitutive element of literature.

3

The specific object of study is space as a component of the literary conceived as historical fact. At the same time, these are hypothetical elaborations in a process of maturation, All study of a historical character is, in good measure, a zeal for ordering, and therefore it is thus that its results are expressed.[9]

Hence, I consider that a first definition of space, interrelated with the historical (with the historical-literary), establishes the role of positioning. Where does this space begin, and where does it end? How is a space defined? What are its components? In fact, the argument now turns on regionalization,[10] where the problem, in which historical "space" is inscribed, begins at the moment one is not able to use common words and concepts. One then must construct next to the specific theoretical edifice the corresponding conceptual scaffolding, so as to give coherence to what is expressed. To simplify, I want to establish that here "region" is understood as the state of Sonora, just as it exists with a basis in the ruling territorial structure of the country. The above does not cancel or obviate the recognition of a greater geographic space in which the region is inserted, which one can call the arid-American ecosystem.[11] The borders of this area are the massive mountains of the southern United States towards the north, Middle America towards the south, the towering mountains of Chihuahua towards the east, and the Sea of Cortez towards the west.

A second moment in the definition of spaces reveals other equally significant elements of a geophysical character that also enter into this definition. In addition to this large territory called the ecosystem, there appears a second topographical division having to do both with the specificity which territorial space achieves in the sphere of a region, and the productive tasks (transformation of nature and society) developed in it. The state of Sonora thus remains divided in four great regions: the south, the coast of Hermosillo, the mountains, and the desert.

One might well say that all space, defined strictly in terms of geography, generates its culture and finally its literature. Not to take into consideration the above leads to an obtuse historicism where the other components of the literary (time, the social) are marginalized, and analysis becomes chronological or sociological.

The importance of space is related not only to the anecdotal contents (most immediately), but also to the roots and antecedents of this anecdotalism and above all to the singularity of language. In a somewhat inverse fashion, Bachelard[12] has offered an analysis of the spatial, since for him what is important is to know which are the essences that break loose from space. He doesn't give much importance to the role that space plays in itself in terms of regionalization. One cannot isolate or depreciate either meaning of space. That is, in spite of the validity of Bachelard's views, and of their broad meaning for the analysis of the problem I have broached here, we cannot consider these views sufficient.

Space (the components of this space) generates topography, society, and culture. With regard to literature, none of these three elements predominates over the others. Rather, it is their interrelation which in one or another form explains the behavior of the concept and of spatial reality. Also, in contemporary times there are two fully aligned kinds of space, although they are increasingly coming into more acute confrontation: rural space and urban space. Of these, the latter tends to predominate, thus causing literature to overlook the former.

As a component of literature, space is differentially manifested in the field of poetry, fiction, and the essay. (Here as well differences exist with Bachelard, for whom space generates unified and non-discriminated essences.) In poetry, space appears as image and naming (the name is born of the concrete-sensible). Narrative space is founded as one part of the story. In the essay space serves as a principle of ordering.

In fact, space does not generate historicity or a historicity of its own. But it is *determining* as historical element. For example, on speaking of "the structures of the environment,"[13] Baudrillard tries to explain how the object—which generally is space or something located there—influences the behavior of the subject. Foucault,[14] on analyzing the limits of the world, knows that the microcosm, as *category of thought,* "applies to all the domains of nature, the game of duplicated resemblances . . ." In the framework of structuralism and in the objectivization of the new French novel, *Tel Quel*[15] knows that these fiction writers and literary writing itself have much to do with distance, aspect, and origin, categories proper to space in which events are developed.

To treat space is to treat a substantive part of literature.

How does Cornejo present mountains in his work? How is the transition from the rural to the urban given in *El norte del milenio*? In Méndez, what predominates, the mountains or the desert? Does space play some role in the poetry of Bojórquez or Manríquez, in the work of Parodi or de la Vara? Where are the writers who incorporate southern Sonora in their work? And Hermosillo? Why its hegemony in contemporary times? What does space communicate to literature? How does it influence and manifest itself in terms of regionalization? Where I end is exactly where the tasks of ordering Sonoran literature begin, through space, tasks I am trying to enter into.

Notes

[1]The argument over the historical has been developed around the correlation of the axes of time and space: the predominance of one over the other. This argument can be amply documented, clearly establishing that history is always time, space, and man in society.

[2]Herbert Cysarz, "Los periodos en la ciencia literaria," in Emil Ermantinger, et al. *Filosofía de la ciencia literaria,* Mexico City: FCE, 1983, p. 109. If indeed Cysarz and the other authors of this book place emphasis on the "philological"—"the creative acts, philologically creative"—in my case I believe that the literary can no longer be reduced to the philological. Instead, on becoming more complex, it requires a broader conceptualization.

[3]More than once, we who live in the provinces have complained of the imprecisions that feed those who approach literature of said provinces from the center. But little in truth, as they would say, is done in the provinces to correct faults and errors. Still, I insist that gradual progress is being made.

[4]An example is the *Historia general de Sonora,* in which literature does not occupy the place it deserves, owing to different causes. Various examples in this respect could be cited.

[5]Wilhelm Szilasi, *Fantasía y conocimiento*. Buenos Aires, Argentina: Amorrortu, 1977. I cite this book because it is one of the most complete to apply Aristotelian ideas to literary questions.

[6]Claude Lévi-Strauss, *El pensamiento salvaje*. Mexico City: FCE, 1972, p. 60.

[7]See Piaget in this connection, who speaks of how thought and action in the child are constructed or nurtured in spatio-temporal terms. Bloch or Augé reflects on the concept of history and how theory and practice of the work are inserted in it.

[8]Cysarz.

[9]Marc Augé, *Símbolo, función e historia*. Mexico City: Grijalbo, 1978.

[10]Octavio Lasuén, *Ensayos sobre economía regional y urbana*. Barcelona, Spain: Ariel, 1976.

[11]*Enciclopedia de la ciencia y de la técnica*, Madrid, Spain: Danae, 1984, pp. 1011-12.

[12]Gaston Bachelard, *La poética del espacio*, Mexico City: FCE, 1983.

[13]Jean Baudrillard, *El sistema de los objetos*, Mexico City: Siglo XXI, 1969, pp. 31-70.

[14]Michel Foucault. *Las palabras y las cosas*. Mexico City: Siglo XXI, 1981, pp. 26-52.

[15]*Tel Quel*, ed. *Teoría de conjunto*, Barcelona, Spain: Seix Barral, 1971, pp. 13-28.

Regional History and Literature: An Endless Essay

> In this war of the spirit of men, the big guns of our armament are, obviously, capacity in languages and in linguistics.
>
> —Newmeyer and Edmonds, *Linguistics and Society*

1

Until now, little thought has been given to the repercussions that the decentralization in process in the country will have on different aspects of the nation's social life. Perhaps this is so because this decentralization goes on being a caricature. In the course of things, on transferring to the states some substantive functions, the processes of social decomposition that already were manifest when centralism was pathogenic have become more acute. That is, for example, the inexperience of the state governments to exercise public power (the case of the opposition governments), or ingrained political-machine schemes of social control, have limited and distorted the federalization of services and functions, thus causing the citizenry frequently to ask whether really decentralization is worth the trouble.

In addition, the truth is that decentralization is in fact in process. It is making relevant the communitarian life that is manifest in the regions of the country. This regionalism, of course, is not identified with the territorial isolation in which the country lived before the processes of national consolidation in the middle of the nineteenth century. It doesn't even have much to do with the social schemes of the Hellenic world or of Medieval Italy, when life in cities was of an incredible spiritual and material richness and when the culture of that period generated products of even universal validity and relevance. An inverse social process is being manifested: in those times energy traveled from the periphery to the center, whereas today the dynamic moves from the center to the peripheries. The task, therefore, is to restore to the latter a cultural power that previously had been down-trodden; peripheries where social exhaustion is seen, and where it is now necessary to construct enduring regional values. Rudolf Rocker (1977: 533) speaks of the Italian cities of those days, saying that they were free: ". . . true oases of high spiritual and social culture, whose surprising multiplicity and creative strength have not been achieved since then." It could be that with decentralization in Mexico, we are moving in that direction. No one of us knows with either precision or certainty, in the case of literature, in spite of the predominance even of heavy centralist schemes, in certain places of the country outside of the Federal District (increasingly so, if we take as an indicator the magnificent independent literary magazines now being published) literary activity is strengthened and produces works of the same intensity and significance as that being created in the nation's center. How do we approach the study of this new literary regionalism? What significance does it have to do so?

2

One of the problems which literary theory has perhaps paid little attention to in Mexico is the non-existence of a national history of our literature which critically approaches the meaning of what has been produced throughout history. In Mexico not a single study (diachronic or synchronic) exists of the continuity of the country's literary history. Fragmentation rules, isolated visions, the study of the individual case, never the visions of the group or of continuity. Is this because it has made no sense to do so? Perhaps, but perhaps also the task is of such magnitude that it would require energies no one could muster. A last possibility is that such a study would simply have to be too ideological, as in fact are those that deal with our history, to the degree that they imply selection, discrimination, and displacements.

That is, if the study of social history is complicated in itself, that of some portions of this history (literature) would be equally so or even more complicated. Hence, we have no comprehensive literary history. Consider the difficulties of attempting such work or answering the question that a group of scholars convoked by Jean-Paul Sartre and Simone de Beauvoir around 1965 put: What is literature for? It is not easy to enter into this material of study, as, for example, Foucault shows in *Las palabras y las cosas* (1981: 289):

> The classical order of language has now been closed upon itself. It has lost its transparency and its great function in the domain of knowledge. In the 17th and 18th centuries it was the immediate and spontaneous development of representations; in it these immediately received their first signs, where their common bonds were cut and retied, where relations of identity or attribution were installed; language was knowledge and knowledge was, with full right, a discourse . . . the things of the world could be understood only by passing through it [language]. . . Through the nineteenth century, language was folded back on itself. It acquires its own thickness, unfolds a history, laws, and an objectivity that belong only to it. It has been converted into an object of knowledge among many others: next to living beings, next to riches and value, next to the history of these happenings and of men.

I believe that in these words of Foucault's the difficulty is enclosed of constructing the history of literature as a group of gears and functions. It implies, among other things, establishing the pace of that which he calls the classical order of language in the framework of a history that if indeed it is a group of arbitrarily fixed correlations, has its temporal and spatial specificities. In other words, it is not the same thing to construct the history of the literature of Spain as that of Mexico, nor that of this country as that of one of its provinces, or that of Baja California as that of Sonora. That is, to construct history is a problem of specificities to be established, in order to generate and to define what has been its social function and that of its components.

Now if we talk of literature, if we indeed speak of language, we are speaking of a specific language perfectly differentiated at least from daily speech, which implies working with different values than those of this daily speech. Then, from that point on, we must differentiate genres and the reason for their temporal and spatial manifestation.

3

What is it that has moved me to ask myself the above questions? On the one hand, there is a knowledge of the literary production of Mexico's northern border, situated in a disorganized but certain course of decentralization of national life. What are its identities and differences? On the other hand, there is the publication of a book by Gabriel Trujillo (1992) which caught my deepest attention, *Un camino de hallazgos,* a gathering of Baja California poems of the twentieth century.

This is the time to talk about the book in its entirety (two volumes, in the first of which we find an introductory essay, meriting attention in this study). The essay interests me especially as it presents the causes and reasons of the selection of the poems. I believe that here—with a rich impressionism[1] (Ginzburg 1989)—various questions are treated dealing with how to approach the history of regional literatures and what it means to do so.

In this respect, I would like to point out the boldness of the selections, making clear the editor's reason or the central criterion on which his work is based: "... the generational differences of the poets which have made it possible" (Trujillo 1992:11). In advance, then, the criterion of selection is founded on something so glib and ethereal as the time of manifestation of the work. Language and space as additional criteria of screening of definition disappear. Why? To what is owed this manifest economy of criteria to complete the task? What implications does this economy have?

I am not here disqualifying Trujillo's work, valuable in various other ways. I am only pointing out the lack of a rigorous methodology with which the study of literature is usually assumed as historical manifestation, at least in the terms of classical order of which Foucault speaks, for whom knowledge is "... infinite accumulation of confirmations which call one to the others" (1981: 39), and which, in the case of literature, require bringing together at least three substantial elements of the literary fact: time, space, and language. Once the presence of these three elements is established, we must consider the correlations and specific weights which each acquires within these relations.

Trujillo's introductory essay made me think that one should not study literature apart from a specific context of time, space, and language on which it is founded. Important considerations here are who emits the messages, who receives them, language and it use, and the group of correlations which are instituted through the elements comprising the circuit of communication generated by the literary object. To study Baja Californian poetry by generation in the way that the author of *Un camino de hallazgos* proposes presents partially and often in a distorted manner the way poetry has historically manifested itself in the twentieth century here. The over-emphasis on time erases the singularity of language and space, thus limiting the reading of the poems contained in the book.

In *De la gramatología* (1984), Derrida calls our attention to the singularity of knowledge inscribed in language, emphasizing the dangers implicit in logocentrism. Decentralization in Mexico today is giving rise to the regional, encouraging us to return to the lessons of Derrida and demand of the study of these regional literatures a much deeper and more precise methodological rigor. The reason for this is so that we do not fall into facile expedients of compiling mere notes that minimize and deny the function of the philologist, for whom "... the text is a deep and invisible entity, which must be reconstructed beyond the facts of the senses..." (Ginzburg 1989:149).

4

If we start from the fact that knowledge is constructed through a group of given premises, and that it is objective "... not only through its own mechanisms of immanent validation, but also insofar as it takes into account the practical-social moment given by its public character, by its submission to discussion by the community. . ." (Manteca Alonso in Edmonds, et al 1976:7), then to study literary phenomena in Mexico, whether in the center or in the regions, undoubtedly demands the existence of a learned reader. Such a reader realizes not only this immanence that language has, particularly from the nineteenth century to the present, but also the full multiplicity of situations proper to immanence, at the same time that they have to do with the social dimension of literature.

The above is situated in the context that decentralization is now constructing and that, among other things, has given it urgency and currency to the dispute over history, understood in its dimension of a referential framework of daily life. There, the schemes founded on hegemonic and centralizing visions having been forgotten and continually questioned, today the construction of new visions is demanded, inside the above-mentioned dispute, which give real, true, certain life to the quotidian prevailing beyond the center of the universe which, in the case of Mexico, means outside the Federal District.

In this context, the construction of regional literary histories is an unavoidable and urgent task. Literary production in Mexico has been constant and continuous not only in the center but also in all the regions of the country. That it has suffered from the pathogenic effects of centralization is certain, but this has not impeded or mutilated it.

Another problem is *how* to write these histories. Some opinions in this respect have been given, taking as point of reference the work mentioned by Trujillo. We should place emphasis on this "how." Within the struggle for history, the project of writing these histories argues strongly for the presence of the peripheries in a country that since the mid-nineteenth century has been ruled by centralizing schemes which have noticeably drowned out life in the provinces.

In the word of Adorno (1962:12), to think in order to write is the basis of construction of the essay: "Luck and play are essential. It doesn't begin with Adam and Eve, but with that which wants to speak; he says whatever it occurs to him to say, stops when he himself feels he has come to the end, and not where nothing more remains . . ." With these notes, I wanted only to begin an essay that I don't even know when or where will end.

References

Adorno, Theodor. *Notas de literatura.* Barcelona, Spain: Ariel, 1962.

Derrida, Jacques. *De la gramatología.* Mexico City: Siglo XXI, 1984.

Edmonds, Joseph, et al. *Lingüística y sociedad.* Madrid, Spain: Siglo XXI, 1976.

Foucault, Michel. *Las palabras y las cosas.* Mexico City: Siglo XXI, 1981.

Ginzburg, Carlo. *Mitos, emblemas, indicios.* Madrid, Spain: Gedisa, 1989.

Rocker, Rudolf. *Nacionalismo y cultura.* Madrid, Spain: La Piqueta, 1977.

Trujillo, Gabriel. *Un camino de hallazgos*. Mexicali, Baja California: UABC, 1992.

Border: Space, Time, and Postmodernity

for Edmundo Valadés, with deep respect

I would have liked to notice that, at the moment I began to speak, a voice with no name had preceded me a long time ago; then it would have been enough for me to link the phrase, to continue it, getting into its interstices without being perceived, as if it had sent me some signals, staying still for a moment. Therefore there would have been no beginning, and instead of being the source of speech, I would have been just a small gap in the hazard of its course, the point of its possible disappearance.

—Michel Foucault, *The Arrangement of Speech*

In the always difficult area of definitions of matters regarding literature, things would seem to be a bit more complicated when reference is made to the new, to that which emerges or has emerged almost out of the immediate present. Such would seem to be the case today now that—for good or ill—border literature is beginning to be known. The argument tends to be increasingly threadbare, in which the main object would be the disqualification of the other, for the pure and simple fact of being "other."

In such a way, trying to negotiate the pitfalls of this Byzantine discussion or of the personalized message, what will be attempted here is to continue examining that question which for some time now we have been posing: in which sociohistoric conditions is literary production on the northern Mexican frontier generated today, and what are the primary characteristics of the work produced? On this occasion, the main idea will revolve around a double reflection on the conceptions of the history of the region itself and literature itself as a social practice.

2

In this sense, in principle, it is necessary to speak in summary about two key concepts—insofar as they impose substantial differences on this region in contrast to others—linked to the border question (needless to say, I refer here to the country's northern border). One, space. Two, time. Thus, space is doubled or folded; on the one hand it has to do with geography, and on the other with history.

In such a fashion, in terms of geography of the northern Mexican border we should concentrate on its ecosystem as substantively different from other ecosystems to be found in the country. The desert region of arid America, where the frontier is found, is radically different from the central plains of the country and the humid tropics that predominate in the southeast. From this the following premise stems, which places emphasis on the fact that the peoples who inhabit a certain ecosystem of necessity create cultures according to the characteristics of these physical environments, which are therefore manifested as different cultures.

It is not gratuitous, then, to speak of the desert if this ecosystem gives rise to the manifestation of the difference. The border, therefore, is essentially different from other areas of the country. In itself, it is different above all if it is horizontally analyzed: in terms of landscape, for example, the east is substantially different from the west, among other reasons because it is closer to the Tropic of Cancer.

In the same way the border, historically speaking, gains singular importance not only on the principle of alterity which is proper and common to all that has limits,[1] but also in the case of the country's northern border this singularity is augmented as a limit that is always in danger, or, if you will, it's a limit under constant tension because the enslaving presence of the United States has been for Mexico a sword of Damocles for some time now.

This alterity in tension is the characteristic that also obliges us to consider the region as a strategic zone for the nation: here, where difference begins, keeping this difference fixed is converted into a priority—and in contrast to national unity—and because of this here can be found a series of diverse activities trying to keep this alterity alive, including, clearly, the questions of diffusion of an art called national.[2] So we hold that by virtue of the geographic space that it occupies the border is a strategic space as much for Mexico as for the United States.

The conception of time I use owes a debt to the way in which Attali[3] links time and history, making us see how a single physical space changes not only in relation to the material transformations it suffers, but also as a function of the social tasks that in it, in this physical space, are discharged.

Time is thus important for this theory of the border beyond the basic transformations signaled by Attali in the time of the Gods, the time of the sacred, the time of bodies, rural time, urban time, and chronometric time. At the minimum we can posit two principles. One, the alterity that emerges establishes a difference: the time of social changes that are registered here (in this case, my contention is restricted to the Mexican border) is different from the time of those changes that are registered in other parts of the country. Decentralization is herewith manifested and uncontainable. Two, alterity as it is marked by borderization, is also marked, in terms of time, by a singular dynamic: present time "runs" more rapidly than that of the past,[4] and it has a determining influence on the manner in which the border is thought of as a sociohistoric space where a specific literature is generated.

3

The border is a sociohistoric space where a specific literature is generated. This observation is located in the interior of the key concepts of time and space. I shall mention three examples that are paradigmatic, and I'll dwell on one of them in particular (these three conceptions of course do not exhaust the existing pool of possible examples in this respect.[5])

In the beginning, I would speak of a conception highly syncretic, although not because of this necessarily eclectic, that emphasizes the impact and influence of Mesoamerican pre-Hispanic cultures as a base of conformation of the specific culture that is generated on the border. Otherness is thus conceived as a resistance in which to survive the Anglo, the "other," the border inhabitant—Mexican or of Mexican origin—accedes to and utilizes "his" culture, which is nothing but the culture of the indigenous, Mesoamerican, pre-Columbian peoples. This is a recycled culture, it is clear, but one that has not lost its roots.

The above-mentioned conception is found in Octavio Paz's book *The Labyrinth of Solitude*,[6] a finished, systematic, solid expression but which in my view does not manage to overcome three limitations. One, he forgets to incorporate into culture the sociocultural traits and elements that create a specific geographic space. Two, it is a static view, in which time, the dialectic, has vanished, dissolved, doesn't appear to perform any function. Three, he forgets that there is a plurality of cultures, and his conception of the border is thus changed into an ethnocentric concept which, I insist, offers nothing to the cultures created in the geographic ambit specific to the border. In spite of this, I recognize that until now such a conception is what has had the most weight and has been the most widespread as a kind of explanation of the cultural phenomena which are created in the region.

The second conception to which I refer is perhaps less organic and systematized than the last, but it has importance because it recuperates an extremely valuable element in terms of the analysis of the social, and which in fact until recently has been overlooked altogether. In this way, said conception[7] on recognizing alterity emphasizes two different ways of conceiving the world depending on the side of the border of the observer. Thus, the Weberian idea of the pragmatic Protestant spirit that characterizes capitalism disappears on confronting the other vision of the world, which dominates on the Mexican side, definitively founded on diverse values, that therefore give origin to forms of behaving, of being, of conceiving life in radically different ways. Thus, the holders of this theory maintain that the border dweller, a being who lives indistinctly in two social worlds, is one absorbed by the *American way of life*) when he lives in the United States and another very different person (bohemian, sloppy, oriented towards the present, spontaneous) when he lives in Mexico. The first is fundamentally Anglo and subjected to capitalist pragmatism. The second more closely fits notions of the ways of life characteristic of the Mexican, according to the authors[8]). Here, the border tangentially divides and thus creates two worlds profoundly different from each other. Each is different from the other; neither is inferior to the other.

A critical view of this conception would perhaps indicate the rigidity of the proposal in which the *ecotone* somehow cancels the porosity of the border and the symbiosis that, in reality, obtains here. In fact, an unequal and unbalanced relation is manifested. However, in the last analysis it is a relation and therefore an interpenetration, an interchange, a mutual influence. Isn't it popularly held, for example, that the Hispanic silently invaded Anglo territory, in particular here on the border?

It is on a third conception of the border that I now want to pause as I believe it is the most current, charged with implications and suggestions.

4

A reading of contemporary reality requires an additional effort to decode the messages which comprise its quotidian aspect. One must take a series of steps to approach the concrete through abstraction—to leave to the side rigid and orthodox paradigms, to begin to work with new theoretical proposals obsessed not with creating light and with pontificating (this is how dogmas are made), to offer proposals that permit the amplification of the work linked to abstraction. At the base of the most recent conceptions of the border[9] are various preoccupations. One of the least explicit is precisely that discussed above, which I mention not to dogmatize but only to offer new elements to the discussion.

Thus, although it is not aggressively, explicitly forwarded as a systematic theory of the border region, the notions of Gómez-Peña, Hicks, and Polkinhorn are located in the area of postmodernity, as I'll attempt to show in the conclusion of this argument. For the present, I detect the following four elements in their conception of the border.

First we have the key concept of borderization in which the limit does not demarcate differences, but it creates an extended space that passes the limit establishing its own, characteristic zone of influence. Here I borrow a concept from ecology to refer to this zone: the ecotone.[10] Two systems, on touching, give rise to a zone of influence between them in which information is methodically exchanged, a syncretism that thus brings about a different zone from those which gave rise to the ecotone. The border of which we here speak is an ecotone zone that extends towards the north of the United States (is Los Angeles not part of the border?) and towards the south in the case of Mexico (La Paz would also be part of this border). This leads us to qualify the ecotone as a sacred zone[11] thatcreates its own life differentiated from the daily. Such a sacralization marks the art work produced here.

The authors mentioned above refer primarily to literature, and because of this we place emphasis on it. That is to say, perhaps it would not be valid to extend this proposal to cover other fields of human activity (economy, politics), but it is also difficult to apply it to other art media. Because of this, the second element that this proposal uses has to do with intertextuality as a basis of the expression of its discourse: visual poetry; iconization of the literary object (be it book or magazine); mixture and syncretization of video, mime, theater, and music; recuperation of oral literature, among other traits, would be concretizing the intertextuality of which this proposal speaks.

A third element is the avant-garde: resistance to and rejection of the traditional and a continual forwarding of options that seek to renovate the bases upon which works of art are created. Thus, the new, the different, is established as a paradigm and a necessity. What's produced on the border does not always share in these features of the avant-garde even though that might have been the intention of the author. Perhaps the attraction has to do with the fact that the avant-garde is in itself a kind of theoretical contradiction[12] which is difficult, almost impossible, to define.

Finally, bilingualism-biculturalism[13] is another key element in this synthesis of features of a border theory. One should not conceive of bilingualism-biculturalism only as a simple mixture of expressions and behavior, but also the emergence of attitudes and new expressions created by the ecotone and its sacralizing character, whose essence, I insist, is a complex exchange of cultures that generates a new culture: border culture, characterized by intertextuality, the avant-garde, and syncresis. In fact, there is a close interrelation and cross-pollination among the elements which make up this proposal.

5

End of the century. End of the millennium. More reflections on human activities. Here, in this border environment we find several key elements of postmodernity.[14] There are those who believe that postmodernity is nothing but the manifestation of a society that is becoming increasingly complex in its daily activities, and that this has led thought, reflection, continually to have to renovate itself. Recuperating here the categories of time and space used in the first part of this argument, one might well say that the border conceived as a sacralized zone originates its own, singular cultural life; it creates its own space and time, which we here characterize as the apparently postmodern.[15]

In this way, postmodern border time and space cover two dimensions, one of a theoretical and the other of a material character. On the one hand—the theoretical—modernity (end of the nineteenth century to the end of the twentieth, through the 1980s) brought about futurism, structuralism, and the negative enlightenment. This lead to postmodernity, whose theoretical discourse is found in poststructuralism (Foucault, Derrida, Lyotard), agnosticism, anarchized Nietszcheanism (de Man and Virilio), and the crisis of academic Marxism (the lucidity in crisis of Habermas).

On the other hand—the material—in modernity macrocephalic urban-centered consumerism, the globalization of everyday life, and the technologization of production thrive. Today postmodernity signals the crisis of the Nation-state (and of the State itself); tendencies that give priority to natural life, to artesanry, and to the resurgence of barter as a option of exchange (all woven together in an intense neoconservative blend).

Located at the extremes—modernity and postmodernity as limit systems—the border ecotone (I reiterate its sacralization) gives rise to another life, inclined towards postmodernity but container even of modernist traits. Because of this, from our vantage point on the border the discourses of modernity sound spent, insufficient to enable a comprehension of contemporary reality. Moreover postmodernity—

evanescent, itself fugitive—would seem to comply with the objective of helping in the full comprehension of everyday life of the region. Can it be that life here in the last analysis remains opaque, beyond explanation, and thus its post-modernity?

References

[1]D. Emily Hicks, "Deterritorialization and Border Writing," *Memoria del Primer Encuentro de Escritores de las Californias*, Mexicali, B.C.: DAC, 1987, pp. 80-9.

[2]The profound contradiction which is created between the strategic character of the region and the predominantly centralizing tendencies is a question on which one has hardly begun to reflect, but whose importance increases daily. Specific studies of such a problematic are scarce, and they usually emphasize questions linked to the economy. Very few deal with culture. I go into this theme more deeply in my study "Para *construir* las culturas regionales," in *Cultura norte,* PCF, Mexico City, 1989, pp. 27-29; published here as *Constructing* Regional Cultures," pp. 79-92.

[3]Jacques Attali. *Historias del tiempo*, Mexico City: FCE, 1985.

[4]This has to do with what Lévi-Strauss said in various of his works: "in terms of change, the first human societies are seen as dominated by synchrony, while current ones are marked by diachrony, which causes changes to be less noticeable in the first while in the second they happen more quickly . . . The societies called primitive bathe in the fluid of history against which they are forced in order to stay impermeable, while our societies interiorize . . . history to convert it into the motor of their development." C. Lévi-Strauss, *Arte, lenguaje, etnología*, Mexico City: Siglo XXI, 1971, p. 34.

[5]I mention here only names: Tino Villanueva, Rodolfo Acuña, Tomás Ybarra-Frausto, David Maciel, and especially the work of Manuel Valenzuela on border subcultures.

[6]Octavio Paz. *El laberinto de la soledad*, Mexico City: FCE, 1964. See here, in particular, "El pachuco y otros extremos," pp. 9-24; in this essay the dichotomy pragmatism/ideality appears already expressed although not totally developed, which will be taken up by García Nuñez and Aguilar.

[7]See Fernando García Nuñez and Ricardo Aguilar Melantzón's small book *La frontera: letra y risa*, Mexico City: UACJ, 1988.

[8]"The Mexican would include a vision of life rooted in the past more than in the future, cemented in fruition and not in the utilitarian, oriented towards the ideals of medieval Catholicism and not towards doubts originated by the Reformation." Ibid., p. 4.

[9]I depart here fundamentally from a basis in the three following texts: Guillermo Gómez-Peña, "Documentado/Indocumentado," in *Memoria del Encuentro de Literatura de las Fronteras*, Mexicali, B.C.: ICBC, 1989, pp. 387-97; Emily Hicks, op. cit.; and Harry Polkinhorn, "Chain Link: Towards a Theory of Border Writing," in *The Line: Essays on Mexican-American Border Literature,* Calexico/Mexicali: UABC/SDSU, 1988, pp. 29-36.

[10]"An ecotone is a transition between two or more diverse communities such as, for example, between forest and meadow or between a coastal community at base soft and another at base hard. It is a zone of union or belt of tension which will perhaps have a considerable linear extension. But it is narrower, in every case, than the areas of the same adjacent communities. The ecotonal community is in the habit of containing many of the organisms of each one of the communities that are characteristic of the ecotone and that at least are confined in it. Frequently, the number of species as well as the density of the population are greater in the ecotone than in the communities which border it. The tendency towards a diversity and a density augmented in the union of the communities is designated as the *edge effect*" (emphasized in the original). E. P. Odum, *Ecología*, Mexico City: Interamericana, 1984, p. 174. In actuality, the *edge effect* is known increasingly as the *effect of the border*.

[11]In a loose sense the sacred would be the non-quotidian, whose texture changes and whose strange function would generate a product, a territory, a prohibited or limited zone (magical in the strict sense), ritual, ceremonial, *distinct.* I am not the first to use this idea; in May of 1989 the Mexican-North American anthropologist David Carrasco articulated the notion in his presentation given as principal speaker at the conference "Border Folklore: A Panoramic Vision."

[12]In an ample arc of possibilities that runs the same from Benjamin to Adorno, from Sollers to Mayakovsky, from Sanguinetti to Paz, I stick, for the purposes of this argument, with the words of Tinianov referring to the avant-garde: "The fundamental notion of literary evolution, of the *substitution* of systems, and of the problem of traditions must be reconsidered from other points of view" (author's emphasis), in *Formalismo y vanguardia*, España: Comunicación, 1970, p. 113. In fact, at the base of all vanguardism lies "substitution" as the motor that dynamizes the phenomenon, and I place emphasis on this here.

[13]It would be necessary to posit—above all in the interior of postmodernity—bilingualism-biculturalism as a territory increasingly more complex but increasingly more real in terms of a border zone (in specific the border zone of which we are talking): an impressive polylingualism, which in an accelerated manner incorporates elements coming from English, Spanish, and diverse variations of Oriental languages (moreover, within each language one should mention the existence and manifestation of dialectal varieties). If indeed this cultural/geographic region marks off borders today, it would not seem too remote one day to see these borders disappear, in Los Angeles and San Diego, in Tijuana and Mexicali.

[14]In a bibliography that is increasingly extending, the following studies are especially relevant for an adequate border theory: Victor Burgin, *The End of Art Theory,* Atlantic Highlands, NJ: Humanities Press International, 1986; Charles Newman, *The Post-modern Aura,* Evanston: Northwestern University Press, 1985.; Paulo Portoghesi, *Postmodern,* New York: Rizzoli, 1983.; Andrew Ross, ed., *Universal Abandon?,* Minneapolis: University of Minnesota Press, 1988; *Art*

after Modernism: Rethinking Representation, New York: The New Museum of Contemporary Art, 1984.

[15]The border, as ecotone, is an island in the interior of postmodernism. It is linked to hegemonized daily life. Postmodernity is not a break with nor a continuity of modernity; hence its frequent recycling of fashion.